THE PASTORS' WIVES' DIARIES

THE PASTORS' WIVES' DIARIES

A Visible Journal of The Invisible Journey

DR. LARRY L. ANDERSON JR.
W/CHRISTINE O. JAMES & MORE

An Anderson and Canty Production

SMS MINISTRIES

Copyright © 2024 by Dr. Larry L. Anderson Jr.

Printed in the United States of America. All rights reserved. No part of this publication may be reproduced, stored in a retrieval system, or transmitted, in any form or by any means, electronic, mechanical, photocopying, recording, or otherwise, except for brief quotations in critical reviews or articles, without the prior written permission of SMS Ministries.

For permissions requests, please contact:
SMS Ministries
2809 W. Stan Schlueter Lp Ste 101
Killeen, TX 76549
info@smsministries.co

Published by SMS Ministries Publishing in Killeen, Texas. First Printing, 2024

SMS Ministries Publishing's books may be purchased in bulk for educational, business, fundraising, or sales promotional use. For information about please email publishing@SMSMinistries.co.

SMS Ministries Publishing is not responsible for the opinions expressed by the authors in this publication. The views and opinions expressed herein are solely those of the individual authors and do not necessarily reflect the views of SMS Ministries Publishing.

Scripture quotations marked (AMP) are taken from the Amplified Bible, Copyright © 2015 by The Lockman Foundation. Used by permission.

Scripture quotations marked (ESV) are taken from the English Standard version ®, Copyright © 1999, 2000, 2002, 2003, 2009 by Holman Bible Publishers. Used by permission. Holman Christian Standard Bible®, Holman CSB®, and HCSB® are federally registered trademarks of Holman Bible Publishers.

Scripture quotations marked (NIV) are taken from the Holy Bible, New International Version. Copyright © 1973, 1978, 1984 by the International Bible Society. Used by permission of the International Bible Society.

Scripture quotations marked TPT are from The Passion Translation®. Copyright © 2017, 2018, 2020 by Passion & Fire Ministries, Inc. Used by permission. All rights reserved. ThePassionTranslation.com.

ISBN/SKU
978-1-7350847-8-7

EISBN
978-1-7350847-9-4

Thank you for seeing us!

Finally, an honest and open look at some very real heart issues of pastors' wives. I am so thankful that Dr. Anderson decided to obey the Spirit's prompting to write a book specifically inspired by the women who stand with their pastor husband and support them in ministry. After serving for 20 years encouraging, coaching, and ministering to church planters and pastors' wives, I expected to read about how women responded to some of the distinctions of being married to a man called by God and ordained in pastoral leadership. I thought I might discover that their stories would be variations of those I had heard before from others. What I didn't expect was a book that could touch the heart and clearly give a sense of El Roi, the God who sees.

This book is not just another pastor's wife's self-help book. While it does include diary entries from pastors' wives on topics of universal experiences, I found the entry paragraphs and closing views from the authors in each chapter to be genuine and most helpful. The difference from other books is that Dr. Anderson is not a pastor's wife, but he is the pastor/husband. His very candid entry for each chapter puts a voice to how many of the husbands may feel when they become aware of their wives' experiences. I believe his testimony can help other men understand how to love, encourage, and bless their wives. The closing view by coauthor Christine James was written with passion and firsthand knowledge of faithful service and the attacks that it brings. I found her to be candid and writing from a heart that made me feel like she knew, and she was hugging you for what you have faced as well, encouraging without coming across like a "just be spiritual about it" attitude. The Scripture verses for personal reflection and the prayer prompts in each chapter were helpful for encouragement and direction. These brought focus to God's sustaining grace through his word and communion with Him for the release of past hurts and motivation toward growth.

I would recommend this book to pastors' wives, church planters' wives, and First Ladies in our churches to help equip them as they walk in unity and obedience to God along with their husbands. I believe that a pastor, church planter, and elder can also benefit from the open, honest view of how the enemy will attack and how we can protect our homes and families so they can thrive in God's Kingdom call. I also believe that any member of a body known as the church should read this book so that they too can learn how to withstand spiritual attacks and encourage their leaders in support and love. I can see this book being used in the kingdom to strengthen and encourage some of the most overlooked, under-appreciated, and often unseen faithful servants in God's Kingdom.

Beth Whitworth *Minister Wives Consultant* **Baptist Resource Network PA/SJ**

* * *

"Diaries are your secret companion and a place where you can be honest with yourself."

The authors have courageously unlocked their diaries so we may have the privilege to learn of their heartaches and heartbreaks as they seek to serve the Lord with their whole hearts. Their stories are real and relevant for discussion and spiritual transformation, whether read individually or in group studies in person or virtually. During the thirty-four years of being a pastor's wife, I witnessed and heard similar experiences from numerous pastors' wives. Paradigms may have changed of being a pastor's wife but the challenges, temptations, and primarily the principles for Godly living have not. This is a therapeutic tool for self-awareness that will result in joyful living in Christ for pastors' wives, pastors and all readers who support kingdom causes.

Sheila Bailey (founding pastor's widow) Concord Church, Dallas, TX

From the moment I started reading, I could not put this book down. As a pastor's wife myself, every entry resonated with me in some way or another. These familiar life experiences took me on a journey. The familiar walk of a heart in private pain, to a heart healing and wrapped in Christ Jesus. The powerful words shared are filled with hope and filled with purpose. They help you to rise, to stand again, and to keep walking in one of the hardest calls of your life. Sis, your pain has a great purpose. It is not in vain. Along with the word of God, this is fuel to keep going.

Shavonya Jarman (pastor's wife) The Influence Church, West Deptford Township, NJ

* * *

Dr. Larry Anderson is a rare servant of God with a unique apostolic perspective on the 21st-century church. Over the years, he has functioned as a church health consultant and author with his hand on the pulse of "what The Spirit is saying to the churches." He and Christine James have collaborated to bring the reader a rare gift—an inside peek into the often isolated world of pastors' wives. They have painstakingly written, procured and compiled the rarely told heartfelt stories of sixteen brave women. This book is a jarring, at times troubling, but riveting collection of behind-the-scenes firsthand accounts of the rigors of pastoral ministry. *The Pastors' Wives' Diaries* is no mere companion book to its predecessor (*The Pastors' Diaries*). It is a stand-alone work as an uncompromising exposé behind the curtain of what goes on in churches nationwide from the persons best equipped to tell it—pastors' wives.

As a pastor, I now have a new perspective. I also have a renewed appreciation concerning my wife, who has faithfully served beside me for over 33 years as my partner in pastoral ministry. Larry Anderson and Christine James are faithful guides into the unknown inner world of some of the world's loneliest people. *The Pastors' Wives' Diaries* is not a book of answers. Yet, it raises compelling questions surrounding how we see and relate to pastors and their wives. This book does not contain easy solutions but rather hard-earned lessons from women whose sacrifices have often gone unnoticed. I highly recommend this book. May this book increase our awareness and empathy toward the church's unheralded heroes and most valuable assets—the pastors' wives.

Paul J. James, Senior Pastor, CareView Community Church

* * *

The Pastors' Wives 'Diaries is a must-read for not only First Ladies but also pastors so they can become more aware of the challenges their wives face and care for them properly. The book reveals firsthand challenges from First Ladies as they stood with their husbands on the front lines of ministry. The transparency of these ladies is a breath of fresh air. However, you will not only hear about the difficult and common struggles these ladies experienced but also how the Lord redeemed all their challenges for His glory and their own good. In addition to the diaries on specific subject matters, the book contains closing perspectives, Scripture reflections, and applicable prayers to help readers navigate these ministry challenges biblically. So, whether you are new to the ministry or a seasoned veteran, *The Pastors' Wives' Diaries* has something for you. I highly recommend this book.

JJ Washington, NAMB National Director of Personal Evangelism

* * *

I cannot express the blessings I experienced reading *The Pastors' Wives' Diaries*. Tears from my broken heart flowed with empathy. Heartfelt diary entries serve as a Balm in Gilead for wives who need healing. The first tear fell reading Pastor Anderson's sincere perplexity regarding the wives who declined his invitation to contribute to this amazing work!

His genuine yet imperative reflections as a man are a clarion call to other pastors' hearts. Christine James' pristine biblical perspectives are a catalyst for wives to move from years of fear to walking in faith for God's glory.

Constance Williams (pastor's wife for 41 years)

* * *

The Pastors' Wives' Diaries is a must-read. I've experienced so many different emotions while reading excerpts of this particular work. I felt guilt, embarrassment, shame, and self-righteousness. Sometimes I put the congregation's needs ahead of my wife. The pastor's wife needs to be valued, honored, heard, considered, seen, and included. Our wives are gifted and called into this work as well. It is also encouraging to know that there are resources available to us to equip us to be the best version of ministry couples we can be. Our wives have wisdom and insight that is valuable to the pastors and congregation. We train pastors for their office and now we can focus on training the ministry team (Pastor and Wife). A must-read.

Pastor Ricky Wilson, Christian Faith Fellowship, Downingtown, PA

* * *

Our feelings and emotions are real. They push us and pull us. They hold us down and they lift us up. They cause us to do the wrong things and they lead us to do great things. Pastors' wives are not exempt from these human experiences. This book may have been intended for pastors' wives, but its message brings empathy and encouragement to all of us. Dr. Larry Anderson has done it again! He has pulled together just the right voices to minister to and enrich all of us.

Mark A. Croston, D.Min National Director, Black Church Ministries Lifeway Christian Resources

Contributors

1. Telisha Acklin, St. James Primitive Baptist Church, Lewisburg, TN
2. Kim Anderson, Great Commission Church, Philadelphia, PA
3. Cynthia Hawthorne Armstrong, Seeds of Greatness Bible Church, New Castle, DE
4. Rebecca Watson Autry, Temple Baptist Church, Fayetteville, NC
5. April Betner, DelVal, East Willingboro, NJ
6. Sharon E. Burton, Baptist Church, Philadelphia, PA
7. Kimberly Coleman, First Baptist Church of Crestmont, Willow Grove, PA
8. Tirzah L. Fontell, Calvary Christian Church, Philadelphia, PA
9. Christine O. James, CareView Community Church, Lansdowne, PA
10. Dr. Melissa Jones LPC, BibleWay Baptist Church, Philadelphia, PA
11. Cynthia W. King, Ezekiel Baptist Church, Philadelphia, PA
12. Vallie T. Kirk, Sharon Bible Fellowship, Latham, MD
13. Cissy McNickle, One Hope Church, Absecon, NJ
14. Tamara Washington, A First Baptist, Church, GA.
15. Shirley A. Wilson, Christian Faith Fellowship, Downingtown, PA

Contents

Foreword   1

From The Authors   3

Introduction   8

JILTED
Contributors   13

Introduction
Larry L. Anderson Jr.   14

The Revolving Door Friend
Dr. Melissa Jones   18

I Hurt
April Betner   22

Is It Me?
Kimberly Coleman   27

Jilted Summary
Christine O. James   32

JEALOUSY
Contributors   35

Introduction
Larry L. Anderson Jr.   36

What About Me?!?
Christine O. James   41

A Journey To Surrender
Cissy McNickle   45

Ride or Die Girl
Kim Anderson   49

Jealousy Summary
Christine O. James   54

JUDAS
Contributors   57

Introduction
Larry L. Anderson Jr.   58

In the Face of Betrayal
Christine O. James   63

The Risk of Trusting
Cynthia Hawthorne Armstrong   67

Judas Among Us
Shirley A. Wilson   73

Judas Summary
Christine O. James   78

JUDGMENT
Contributors   81

Introduction
Larry L. Anderson Jr.   82

Falling Forward
Tamara Washington   85

Judgment, No Judgment
Telisha Acklin   89

I Come Not to Judge Cynthia W. King	93
It Comes with the Job Rebecca Watson Autry	98
Judgment Summary Christine O. James	103

JEZEBEL

Contributors	107
Introduction Dr. Larry L Anderson Jr.	108
Encountering Jezebel Christine O. James	113
A Spirit of Jezebel Vallie T. Kirk	118
Suburban, Not Stupid Kim Anderson	123
Jezebel Summary Christine O. James	128

JOY

Contributors	131
Introduction Larry L. Anderson Jr.	132
The Search for Joy Tizrah L. Fontell	136
Despite My Losses, I Still Have Joy Sharon E. Burton	139
Joy for the Journey Shirley A. Wilson	144

The Joy of Serving
Telisha Acklin   149

Joy Summary
Christine O. James   153

A Question   155
Other Works   157
About the Authors   159

Foreword

I experienced sheer joy when I was invited to learn from my fellow sisters who are also "Pastors' Wives." I was blessed to hear of the known and unknown challenges and struggles, to read about pain, patience, perseverance, and yet, still have JOY!

Praise God for Dr. Larry Anderson and Kim Anderson for listening and responding to the call. The life experiences and lessons within each page of *The Pastors' Wives' Diaries* are so needed.

As I write this, I am still emotionally impacted but also spiritually encouraged by what was shared. To give you an idea of the benefit and impact that will be experienced through reading and embracing the book, allow me to share a glimpse of quotes that left me with moments of "oh my goodness."

> "When people are done, God isn't"

> "Excellence can be confused with perfectionism and overwork."

> "Gifted people with good intentions can be troublesome if their gifts are not yielded to the Holy Spirit."

> "The antidote to unhealthy destructive judgement is the presence of God."

> "The next time we are tempted to judge one another, let us breathe together. Grace in, Grace out."

> "When you let God in the hard places of your life, you are surrendering all to Him."

The assignment and responsibility of being a healthy helper (wife) to the one who responds to God's call of being a pastor is not for those who are not willing to be strongly rooted and grounded in the Word of God. This book reveals the practical and emphasizes the importance of growing and developing a relationship with the Lord. Each chapter concludes with summaries, scriptures and prayers that help us focus and be specific during our time of healing and restoration.

Dr. Anderson and Sister Christine, I am grateful for your obedience and diligence in bringing us this EXCELLENT WORK. Thank you for remembering those who stand beside and with pastors as their wives and life ministry partners. Thank you for seeing us and making space for our journey.

Well, done, thy good and faithful servant.

And whatever you do, whether in word or deed, do it all in the name of the Lord Jesus, giving thanks to God the Father through him. -Colossians 3:17

Dale Patrica Sharpe-Lee
Wife of Rev. Dr. Paul R. Lee
Jones Memorial Baptist Church, Philadelphia, PA

From the Authors

Dr. Larry L. Anderson Jr.

Welcome to *The Pastors' Wives' Diaries*, my follow-up to *The Pastors' Diaries*, published in 2022. Let me start by saying this book is designed to bless the entire body of Christ. Yes, our First Ladies will courageously share their diary entries—a therapeutic journey for them and a testimony of validation for pastors' wives all over the world—but in addition to pastors' wives sharing their stories, the pastors themselves will have an opportunity to sit and listen to the hearts of the women who deeply love them and have made amazing selfless sacrifices to serve their pastor-husbands and the church.

The body of Christ will get a special behind-the-curtain peek into these women's journeys. They will encounter a perspective deeper than the superficial views our ladies typically display while under watchful eyes. Now, you get to hear about the rich and often painful encounters that fostered these women's actions. I want to thank these courageous women authors who said yes to God and allowed themselves to be used to bless the body of Christ.

Because this book began as a nudge from my wife, I want to thank her for the challenge she placed on me to recognize the plight of the pastor's wife. This book is dedicated to you, Kim, as I still cannot fully comprehend the position you have been placed in and the experiences you have had to endure over the last twenty years of ministry.

I thank you for your grace and your unending love and support in our ministry. In the words of the famous songwriter Bobby Womack, "(No Matter How High I Get) I'll Still Be Lookin' Up to You."

Thank you to Leanora Conner for serving as my publishing admin and helping to see this book go from a future vision to a present contribution to the body of Christ to bless the Lord. Thank you for being my liaison and ambassador between all our women contributors and myself.

Thank you to my prayer warriors, Sisters Barbara Durant and Brenda Holton, for agreeing to pray this book through from conception to completion. Although spiritual warfare was present, I believe it was kept from being victorious due to your prayerful intercession.

Thank you to those faithful individuals who took the time to read, review, and endorse this work before its release: Beth Whitworth, Sheila Bailey, Shavonya Jarman, Paul J. James, J.J. Washington, Constance Williams, Ricky Wilson, Mark A. Croston, and Dale Patricia Sharpe-Lee. All of your words of wisdom and encouragement were truly inspiring.

Thank you to my editor, Shana Murph, as we just completed our third project together. It is always a blessing to work with you.

Thank you to my Sister, Christine James, for joining me in this writing experience. You were such a blessing to work alongside during this journey. Having you as a coauthor immediately brought a spiritually tender, mature, and experiential perspective to the room that I desperately needed to help this book come to fruition.

Finally, I just want to thank you, Jesus, for doing it again. You never cease to amaze me. You continue to remind me that this work that you began in me, you will carry it on to completion.

You have continually given me a platform to lovingly examine your fellowship, expose the foul, encourage the faithful, and edify the flock. To God Be the Glory!

> *A wife of noble character who can find?*
> *She is worth far more than rubies.*
>
> Proverbs 31:10 (NIV)

Christine O. James

When Dr. Anderson invited me to be a co-author of this very important book, I felt both gratitude and deep anticipation about what God was seeking to do on behalf of pastors' wives, as well as apprehension about what it would be like to tell real, authentic stories from the heart. I shed tears of great humility that God would trust me to undertake such a project.

Pastors' wives are not often encouraged to talk about their reality as they come alongside the men God has called. The deep reverence that people often give to the men of God is not necessarily given to the partner walking alongside him. At best the wives may be appreciated for the gifts they bring to help in the pastors' work, but at its worst, wives are often expected to be the silent partner who is to show up poised and polished and quietly remain in what is at times an invisible space.

After over thirty-two years as the wife of a pastor, I have walked with women in leadership and, more specifically, with pastors' wives as a leader in a prayer summit movement held specifically for pastors and their wives. That ministry, as well as personal mentoring and counseling, has given me the opportunity to share my stories and laugh and cry with these women as they share their own.

My personal preference usually consists of putting away some of the difficult stories in favor of trusting God for a brighter future. As I began to write and pour out my stories, I would find myself coming to an abrupt halt, removing my fingers from the keyboard and reflecting, "Is this a safe story to tell? How will people respond to this story?" But ultimately, I pressed on. I pressed on because I wanted to give to others what I prayed for during turbulent or uncertain times on my journey. I wanted someone to share their story with me to help me to understand my own. I longed for someone who would be transparent in their sharing and not just shush me up in the protection of my husband's role as pastor.

How grateful I am for Dr. Anderson and his precious wife Kim. Their private conversations about the plight of the pastor's wife have ignited a fresh vision for a tool that could be a tremendous encouragement to those in the role of the pastor's wife, their pastor-husbands, and the communities they serve. I am also very proud to be named among this group of courageous women who agreed to be contributors to this project. Every story matters. Every point of joy, pain, or sorrow has become a part of the tapestry woven together by God to make us all look more like His Son.

Thank you to my dear partners in prayer (you know who you are). You warrior women are such a gift to my life. Your discerning prayers for me and for all involved in this project covered us so we could keep moving in the midst of ongoing spiritual warfare.

To the very talented and loving group of humans lovingly called The "Justincredibles," I deeply love you and appreciate you for all of your prayers and support during this project. Watching you all walk out your creative callings each day inspires me to keep moving forward into all that God has called me to be.

And finally, my heart is overwhelmed with gratitude for the tremendous man to whom I am married, Paul J. James. His visionary leadership as a shepherd after God's own heart has inspired me, challenged me, empowered me, and given me the courage to live authentically in every area of my life. Thank you, honey. I will love you forever.

My hope is that those who read through these pages will do so with open hearts and minds, praying all along the way. Praying that God will continue to perfect us as His people, His body, helping us all to more deeply reflect His love that never fails.

Introduction

DR. LARRY L. ANDERSON JR.

From the moment I began working on my second book, *The Pastors' Diaries*, my wife made a sly comment about when the pastors' wives' diaries would be coming out. I dismissed her comment and went on to explain to her the state of pastors today. I shared with her the challenges of the position. I further told her, "Until you sit in this seat, you have no real clue of the overwhelming call we have on our lives." I shared the troubling statistics of diminutive pastoral tenures and the countless pitfalls pastors have experienced that have taken them not only from their churches but out of ministry altogether. I shared how I wanted to shed light on this epidemic and bring transparency to the pulpit so awareness and healing could begin to take place in the body of Christ. She listened to me politely and then said something like, "And you don't have any idea what it feels like to be one of those pastors' wives." This time I didn't dismiss her comment as if it was not true. I acknowledged that she was right and I did not know what their wives were experiencing. I then attempted to move on, wondering why she was hating on this new book I knew God was calling me to write. To be clear, I was not discounting that a pastor's wife had to endure some challenging circumstances, but I honestly and quietly thought that it doesn't compare to what pastors go through.

Fast-forward to book signing number one: Great Commission Church is packed with our esteemed authors and distinguished guests. The buzz was great, as it was obvious the crowd in attendance loved the book and eagerly engaged the authors. I was surprised at how many people had already read the entire book, as it was released less than two months prior. However, the transparent stories of our authors had really touched the body at large and they were very passionate about sharing their thoughts on the diaries. We opened our official gathering with each author in attendance reading a snippet from their diary entry. We shared some of the amazing reviews that were posted on Amazon as well as the publisher's page. Then it happened, the moment we opened up the room for Q & A, someone asked, "When is the pastors' wives' diaries coming out?" I responded with, "It's interesting you should ask that, as I have heard that first from my wife and now from a few others. However, I have to see what God has to say about it." One week later we are in Coatesville, Pennsylvania at our second book signing. It almost seemed like a rerun of the first. There was a true appreciation for *The Pastors' Diaries,* but somehow it shifted to a question concerning the writing of the pastors' wives' diaries. The following week I was in North Carolina at another book signing and déjà vu happened again. Subsequently, each book signing, podcast appearance, lecture, and interview, all seemed to have similar thematic trajectories to the wives' diaries. What I originally received as a sly comment from my wife or a lack of sensitivity to what the Lord had produced in me in *The Pastors' Diaries* was now this blaring gong telling me I must affirm this unspoken narrative of the pastors' wives.

Over the next year, I began engaging many pastors and their first ladies about the idea of writing a diary featuring the pastors' wives. There was a unanimous consensus that this was something that desperately needed to be written. I was informed that as lonely and isolated pastors might have been, their wives were facing an even greater level of isolation. When I questioned how that was even possible, I was reminded that at least pastors have each other, as well as other outlets, resources, and support systems to care for us. Whether we as pastors take advantage of these things is entirely up to us, but at least there are retreat centers, counselors, and books upon books to our avail. However, I was told the pastors' wives often do not even have each other to confide in. I was also informed that the resources that are out there for the wives do not deal with the plight of the wife; rather it tells them how to be an even better and godlier woman to complement their husbands and serve their churches. One wife even said the church forces them to look more like *The Stepford Wives* than the human vessels they were called and created to be.

Following these countless conversations, I became convinced that a resource was needed to serve these women directly and the church at large. However, I was not convinced it was my assignment. I was planning to write a second entry to *The Pastors' Diaries* because of the overwhelming response to the book and the plethora of pastors who contacted me following its release to share that they had a story to tell and a desire to be heard as they believed their journeys could be a blessing to the body of Christ. I sought the Lord in prayer for direction concerning what was next, and I felt I was being led to recruit some pastors' wives, affectionately known as "First Ladies," for this next project. Of course, not being a pastor's wife, I definitely could not attempt to *wifesplain* to wives, so I needed to make sure it was their voice explaining their plight.

This is where the difficulty began. The wives unanimously agreed this project was needed but when asked to participate in sharing their stories, the amount of declines I received was mind-blowing. Women with many years of experience who even led various events for women in general and pastors' wives emphatically declined. This was the exact opposite of what I was expecting. In fact, when I approached the pastors for *The Pastors' Diaries*, I was expecting some reluctance, and yet they were more than eager to participate, so much so that I had to place a ceiling on the entries because there were just too many. However, because of the overwhelming resistance of these women, I now found myself asking God if I really did hear from him. Is this not what you said was next for me? I began to speak to some of the women who said yes and those who said no and questioned the resistance I was getting. Their responses are what made me know this book had to be written.

One woman told me, "My husband would never allow me to share my story." Another said, "I cannot bear to relive that pain again," and yet another shared, "The body already sees us as the wicked witch, I cannot participate in my own polarization," and "I really wish my husband and the body was ready to hear our story and love us the way we need to be loved and serve, but unfortunately we are expected to be silent and smile and to share my story would only lead to more criticism and I just cannot handle anymore." I received many more stories and legitimate reasons for why women were choosing to remain silent, and I came to realize that it was quite possible this book may have been needed even more than *The Pastors' Diaries*.

Throughout this book, I will write an introduction to each chapter for a couple of reasons. First and foremost, I have to admit through my dialogue with all of these first ladies, I was being convicted by the Holy Spirit for the role I played, albeit unknowingly, nevertheless guilty, in my wife's pain. I was embarrassed that after 19 years of pastoring and truly believing I was doing a great job of shepherding and protecting my wife, I came to discover I had come up short of covering her the way she needed. I had no idea how deeply I would be impacted by this discovery process, and I had to repent to my God and apologize to my wife for my personal failures. I am not one to hide from my shortcomings, as I hope my transparency can only lead to others examining themselves and growing from what the Holy Spirit reveals to them. Coincidentally, when I asked the ladies if this book should even be written by me or by them alone, I received a unanimous yes. Not because I was the perfect husband or pastor but the exact opposite was their reasoning. It was because I was honest about my failures and my willingness to bare my soul alongside their personal stories. These women felt that in order to ensure their stories would not be viewed or dismissed as a book written by women for women, they desired my pastoral transparency and support. They wanted the "Diaries" brand backing them to broaden the readership to include pastors and the body of Christ.

Finally, I pray this book brings awareness and sensitivity to the women who serve their pastor-husbands and the bodies they've been called to pastor. I pray for the healing and reconciliation of broken relationships between pastors' wives, their husbands, and their churches. And finally, I pray for my sisters who are in bondage and feel like prisoners in their own churches where there should be joy. I pray they find liberation and affirmation, and that this book can be a tool to help create that reality. Amen.

JILTED
Contributors

Introduction
Dr. Larry L. Anderson Jr.

The Revolving Door Friend
Dr. Melissa Jones

I Hurt
April Betner

Is It Me?
Kimberly Coleman

Jilted Summary
Christine O. James

Introduction
Dr. Larry L Anderson Jr.

One feeling that invaded my home more than any other is jilted. For those of you not familiar with the term "jilted," it can be synonymous with rejected, ditched or abandoned. When we say Christianity is not about religion but about relationships, we know that those relationships define what we have with God and one another. Loving God and loving our neighbors as ourselves is what the church family is built upon. When taken seriously and biblically, church is not where we go; it's who we are. We are not just friends from church, but we are brothers and sisters in Christ.

 If there is ever a person who embraces the familial understanding of the body of Christ, it will be my wife. Kim is Miss Extrovert, and her personal tagline, which she says almost every week in service, is "We are a church who loves God and loves people," and she means it. Everyone remembers and still brings up the time when our church went on a retreat and the only person who was able to name everyone who attended was my wife. There have been people who visited our church one time and came back years later, and somehow Kim still remembers their names. Because of her gift of hospitality and her extrovert temperament, Kim organically became the head of the church's Greeter's

Ministry. She stands at the door every Sunday, greeting members and visitors alike as they enter the sanctuary. She is attentive and sensitive in trying to keep families seated together and directing guests to places where they would feel more comfortable during worship. She does not have a problem asking a long-standing member to relinquish their seat in order to accommodate a guest. Most people are amazed when they find out she's the pastor's wife because they have a caricature of what the first lady is like and Kim does not fit the tight mold they imagined. I gave you this extensive description of my wife so you can understand how the one who loves so hard and is willing to go all in on a relationship can also be the one who experiences pain in such deep ways.

When Kim and I started dating, she had a crew of girlfriends. However, over the years as she got closer to me and closer to the Lord, each one of them disappeared. This maturing and moving on is natural for most of us, but for Kim, it was very painful. She still mourns the friendship and the closeness she believed she had with those ladies. Although she had God, a husband, and eventually children, her ideal scenario was to have her friends grow old with her.

Now we are pastor and first lady, and at Kim's suggestion, we try to take every new couple to dinner to welcome them to our church and to give them at least one personal moment outside of the building with us. These encounters are challenging for me because although I am cordial and welcoming to our new members, a part of me is acutely aware that this couple who is here today can be gone tomorrow. However, Kim believes if we love them enough, check on them enough, encourage them enough, then we will be able to keep them forever, and herein lies the challenge. See, I know no matter how great we are to our members, they can decide to leave the church for reasons that have absolutely nothing to do with us. And the sad part is that it does not matter how much we invested in them. Somewhere in their minds they believe it was our duty to do so, and therefore. they don't even owe us a "goodbye we're leaving" as they walk out the door.

No matter how much I attempted to resist, Kim and I have had deep personal relationships in the church. It happened. We became not just friends but best friends with another couple in the church. It's rare to find a couple where the husbands and wives become best friends individually and corporately. They were not just our favorite couple to hang out with; the wives were best friends and talked daily, and the husband and I were best friends. We hung out all the time as well. Our double dates turned into weekend getaways that morphed into summer vacations together. Up until this point in ministry, Kim and I had gone about ten years without having true friends who we could share our lives with, so this was a refreshing turn of events.

This friendship went on for over a decade and was a true blessing in our lives. However, as the saying goes, all good things must come to an end, and yes, the precious friendship that we enjoyed so much ended. Unlike other jilted situations where you are ghosted and left wondering what happened, we knew exactly what happened and it had nothing to do with Kim or me, and yet we still lost our best friends. I was disappointed, of course, but I also understood that sometimes people are not able to function normally alone and are not in a position to be faithful friends to others. However, Kim was devastated. She felt that if there ever was a time to be a friend, it's when you feel the most devastated and desire to be isolated. To this day Kim has not recovered from this hurt and has finally joined me in never wanting to have personal relationships in our church ever again.

Imagine the loneliness the pastors' wives experience. They are surrounded by people all the time but so keenly aware that getting too close to the people can hurt. Ironically, having no close relationships with people does hurt. I'm not sure there is another place in the world where people can become such an intimate part of your life and yet disappear from your life so frequently. I have loved people and have shared my life with them, knowing I may never get anything in return, even though I know the Lord will one day reward me. I've blessed folks with living room and dining room sets, a car and even offered my mother's house to a family facing homelessness, and regardless of the sacrifice offered, I recognize folks will use, abuse, and then remove themselves from your life. I say this to say I could easily walk around bitter as if the world owes me something, but I recognize it's unto Jesus I'm always in debt. Every blessing I have been able to share is to the glory of my Lord.

So, if you are a pastor's wife reading this, please be encouraged. Please know your love is not in vain. Please know you are more like Jesus than you could ever imagine. Jesus knew everyone He ever met would sin against Him. Jesus knew while we were yet sinners, He would die for us. Jesus knew the best of what people had to offer Him was still just filthy rags. And although our sins are as red as scarlet, He knew He would cleanse us white as snow. So, celebrate who your Savior is, and please consider it pure joy when you face trials of many kinds and from many people, knowing that the testing of your faith will produce perseverance. In addition, don't you stop being yourself and loving on people because through these tests you will grow into complete maturity and will lack nothing.

The Revolving Door Friend
Dr. Melissa Jones

Dear Diary, I cannot begin to count the many times, as a pastor's wife, I have experienced the pain of what I thought was a true friend leaving the church. She abruptly cut off our relationship without any explanation and with no opportunity for closure. In 1993, I was twenty-four years old when my husband was called as the second pastor of the Bible Way Baptist Church in West Philadelphia. As of 2024, we have served Bible Way for 30 years. Many have described my role as "a high calling and a high privilege." I remember feeling super excited to serve God in this way because I had great examples of other pastors' wives who modeled grace and dignity in their roles, like Mrs. E. Lynn Reed of Sharon Baptist Church and Mrs. Patricia Richardson of Christian Stronghold Baptist Church, both of Philadelphia, Pennsylvania and later Dr. Lois Evans of Oak Cliff Bible Fellowship of Dallas, Texas.

I felt blindsided and surprised when, almost immediately after becoming a pastor's wife, I was met with harsh criticism. My role and accompanying expectations were as many as they are to this day. In the beginning stages of ministry, I noticed my age intensified the lack of respect I received from many who saw me as too young for such a role.

I quickly learned the seat for which I longed and felt privileged to fill was one of the loneliest positions in the church.

Many times, I received advice from seasoned pastors' wives warning me to avoid friendships with church members. But for me, a bubbly, extroverted person, hearing and applying this wisdom from my elders was an extremely difficult thing to do. I found it incredibly challenging for me to suppress my desire to be close friends with the ladies of our church because, after all, I spent much of my time serving and working with them. I tried very hard to avoid friendships with church members, but what made it even more difficult to avoid these relationships was my inability to connect with other pastors' wives because they, too, were busy. Spending time together with fellow pastors' wives was, therefore, infrequent.

Some years later while pursuing my master's degree at Philadelphia Biblical University in Langhorne, Pennsylvania, my belief system surrounding friendships in the church was challenged. I remember participating in counseling laboratory classes and writing the words: "I am a pastor's wife, therefore I do not have the privilege of letting my guard down; that I must stay distant and keep my family safe from the members." To my surprise, my Christian professors often gave me poor grades on my own personal reflections (after all, I was training to be a counselor/therapist). I can still hear them saying, "You cannot take anyone where you are unwilling to go yourself," and "It is more freeing to love than it is to be guarded." I thought, "What in the world?" Every strategy I used to protect myself was now being challenged and needed to be changed according to them.

As I continued to serve alongside my husband and in my role as the Director of the Women's Ministry, my invisible wall began to collapse, allowing members into my personal space and heart. Once my wall of protection was removed, I assumed if I fellowshipped with women, invited them over and trusted them with the vulnerable places of my heart, they would, in turn, love me at the same level that I loved them.

I believed I was modeling the biblical principles of the Titus 2 woman by discipling others, providing a listening ear when needed, caring for them and even meeting some of their material needs. I kept pressing my way, doing what I thought was the "Lord's work" because I was loving on HIS people, even if they did not love me with the same intensity with which I loved them.

To be honest, it felt good not to have to worry about keeping my guard up. It felt freeing to love others no matter the role or position I served. Spending time with the ladies provided me with an opportunity to have adult conversations apart from raising my children and my normal routine. I was tired of feeling lonely.

I trusted many church members over the years. Of course, I continued to do these things because I had a strong desire to serve God (believing above all else I was to love others more importantly than myself). I was a friend to many, assuming they were also friends to me. Now, as I reflect over the past 30 years, I chuckle due to the realization that the experiences were repeatedly the same. Someone would pursue me, saying, "God called me to assist you," or they would be nice to me, talk to me, laugh with me, go out to eat with me, you name it until they were close enough to see my humanity and then they became distant.

I can recall hearing individuals say things like, "I'm never leaving the church. We love you and Pastor. We love your kids. God is calling me to serve you both. Let me help you. When can I come over? I'm here for you. I have a gift for you. I can do it better than someone else." Constantly hearing these phrases made it difficult to trust others, and once again, my wall of protection, which I tore down, was built back up. Many expected me to be available despite issues I was experiencing within my own world. My husband and I were raising four children, pursuing our education, and burying our parents. The stress of the ministry weighed on our marriage, and our battle with health issues became unbearable at times.

Our greatest pain in ministry was a result of members who befriended us and our children and later left the church (without any discussion with us). They ultimately blamed my husband and me for their departure. My husband and I were so friendly to the members that some had our personal phone numbers and even knew where we lived. This was rare because many pastoral couples did the opposite. We made ourselves available to members, but they would leave the church without any real explanation, at least to us. We never had a chance to tell our story fully, if at all. We were not extended the same grace others expected us to extend.

Each incident made us even more vulnerable. We made the mistake of sharing pieces of our story with the next set of individuals who pledged their loyalty to God and us, only to have the same experiences happen again. These were the same individuals who said they loved us. We were hurt again, and others who had never experienced this kind of leadership role could not comprehend why it bothered us so much. The pain was heavy and even excruciating at times. Ultimately, we had to lean into our faith and commitment to our God to remain steadfast in this journey of ministry. So now, thirty years into this seemingly unending, painful part of the cycle of ministry, I am learning to be still because God is the only one who can truly satisfy the deepest longings in my soul.

I Hurt
April Betner

Dear Diary, This is one of the reasons why I never wanted this job. I didn't ask for this. I never asked to be a pastor's wife. I married my soulmate, the man of my dreams, the love of my life, and he was NOT a pastor when I married him. To be honest, being a pastor's wife was the last thing I ever wanted to be. I saw too much growing up in church. No way was I signing up for that. Yet...somehow, I wound up in this place. I married a man who discovered a pastoral call on his life AFTER I married him. And when he was called, did anyone ask me if it was okay? NO! My opinion doesn't trump the call or hand of the LORD—even I knew that. Even if I wanted to tell him, "No, don't do it," I could never in good conscience do that. I, too, recognize the call of the Lord on his life, but to be honest, moments like this make me want to beg him to call it quits. This is the painful part of being the "First Lady" that no one talks about. Even though I knew this was coming, hearing it still makes me sad. I keep hearing those words of wisdom, "When God gives vision, He doesn't give names." Yet, it's human nature for us to want to envision the future and oftentimes, we put names and faces to the vision.

As God brings people in and we become aware of their gifts, walk with them, disciple them, and give them an opportunity to use their gifts, we can easily start to see them in the future life of the ministry. So, when people tell you they are all in, this is their church, God sent them here, and they are in it for the long haul—only for them to turn around and tell you what feels like weeks later—that the Lord is leading them to transition out...that's tough! Their names were in my husband's vision for the ministry for the long haul! They are full of potential, and I watched him pour his life into them, without restraint or complaint, and he did it with joy. It wasn't a burden for him. And although he puts on a brave face, I know that deep down inside, this hurts him. I know that deep down inside, he knows that he has more pouring to do, more discipling to do. What do you do when folks are done with you and the ministry, but your heart isn't done pastoring them? How do I, as his wife, help him navigate that all while dealing with my own pain? When he let them in, WE let them in. Yes, he is the pastor, but I am his wife and we are one. He preaches and pastors, and I love the people and lift them up in prayer. We are a team. Whatever impacts him impacts me, and vice versa. We embraced these folks as family and now we have to say goodbye. Granted, I appreciate their efforts to "leave right" and have a conversation with us instead of just disappearing without a word like some others (even those in leadership) have done. However, I can't help but question the motive behind even this decision to talk to us beforehand. I can't help but make the connection between them informing us that they are moving on and the online post we recently shared about healthy transitions when leaving a church.

I'm grateful they aren't leaving abruptly without a word or warning as others have done. Some people leave without a word or final goodbye to the congregation. They are there one Sunday and gone forever the next Sunday without a word. So yeah, I'm grateful for them telling us and giving us a heads-up, but it still hurts. On top of that...I can't help but wonder, "Why?" Like what makes you want to leave now? Why didn't you leave when we moved from the old building location to the new location? We naturally lost members during the transition—that would have been a perfect out. Why and why now??? Was it something we did? Was it something that we didn't do? Don't just tell me God is leading you elsewhere. What's the REAL reason you are leaving? The pain of silence here is grueling. Being denied the other side of the story, the truth behind the decision to transition is difficult, especially when we know there have been conversations outside of us with other members. The only question I want an answer to is, "Why are you leaving?" Accepting their canned response while knowing there is more to the story is difficult at best. Is it bad for me to want to know why? Is there an unrealistic sense of entitlement? Do they owe their pastor, his wife, or the church they've served an explanation? What would "knowing" do for me? I don't know the answers to any of these questions, and from the looks of things, I never will. I have to find comfort in the silence, rest in what is unresolved and somehow find peace.

The toughest part about this "break up" is that I have to keep quiet and protect their reputation while I wait for their departure. There's no one for me to talk to about this or confide in. I am left to process this situation, the questions, the confusion, and the pain by myself. I mean, yes, I have my husband, but honestly, he seems 100 percent okay with this. When I tried talking to him about it, he told me it was okay because the Lord showed him it was coming. He also said that he appreciated the fact that they came to him and told him face-to-face that they were leaving and wanted to put a transition plan in place. They also expressed appreciation and gratitude for their time in the ministry and for his investment in them. Now, that's all well and good, but none of that addresses my hurt, my frustration, or my pain. I am hurt because I let them into the sacred space of my heart as their first lady, and no one (not even the LORD) has told me anything in advance. While my husband had a relationship with the man, I had a relationship with his wife, but she has said absolutely nothing to me about any of this. Is it wrong for me to want to hear from her directly? Is it wrong of me not to want her to have the convenience and privilege of hiding behind her husband on this one and letting him be her covering? Right or wrong, I feel like she owes me a conversation, woman to woman.

Anyway, I don't want to tell my husband how I feel because it seems like he is in a good place. He was laughing and joking with the people after the meeting at church today. He's good and I don't want to pull him down. I also don't want to make him feel like he shouldn't have confided in me about the situation or that I am too fragile to handle things like this. I want him to be able to tell me things like this because I am his partner in life. I just wish there was a way for us to talk through it where I can process with him how I feel without coming across as spiritually immature, too emotional, or like I'm doing too much. Maybe he and I can have a conversation sooner than later, but for now, I have a safe place right here with you—my journal and pen. You never judge me. You allow me to be free to think, feel, vent, and process without restraint.

So...where do I go from here? I know that pain is an inevitable part of the human experience, especially when you have more than one human with another. I also know that transitions are normal and natural. We are here now, but we may very well find ourselves in this place again, so how do I guard my heart in the process? Do I completely close off my heart to the people in our church? Do I put up walls and barriers? How do I prevent myself from being heartbroken again?

Here's what I know: God has called us to community—knowing full well that we would be hurt in community, yet He calls us still! So no, I can't put up walls or block people out. I must balance, remaining a conduit of God's love all while having healthy boundaries IN community. God also calls us to Himself—so although wounded in the community, there is a safe place where I can receive healing and strength and grace to return BACK to the community and minister love like I've never been hurt. I also know that I need to walk in wisdom and have boundaries. The people in our church aren't my friends. This can't be a place where I build my friend base. I can be friendly to them, yes, but they aren't my friends. Living by this principle will be freeing for me and them because it will help me have healthy and realistic expectations. So, while I may not be able to prevent this situation from occurring in the future, I can definitely do a better job of making sure my heart and soul are better prepared in the future. I can and I will. For now, I will just ride this thing out—lay here in bed and deal with it as best I know how—Journal. Pray. Sleep. Repeat.

- Jaded Jill

Is It Me?
Kimberly Coleman

Dear Diary, here we go again. I've been working hard—planning, arranging, praying. I thought I had all my ducks in a row. Now, it's the week of our church's Women's Weekend, and I find myself scrambling to fill a void yet again.

I am reminded so vividly of the first time I was in this situation. My husband had only been pastoring for five years, and I was still trying to figure out how to navigate life as a pastor's wife. This new role as "first lady" was in addition to that of wife, mother, part-time seminary student, and full-time accountant. That particular year, I also assumed the task of leading our women's ministry. My assistant servant leader and I were busy with the task of planning our first biannual retreat. This was a major undertaking that would take a lot of planning and coordination. A venue needed to be secured, themes and colors would have to be selected, an itinerary and speakers to be considered and you know the ladies better leave with a great swag bag! This would be a challenge for anyone, to be sure, but I was feeling extra pressure (much of it self-imposed) because I was the pastor's wife. Certainly, the success of this event would be a reflection on not only myself but my husband as well.

Once the location was secured and deposits were paid, my co-laborer, Sarah, and I divided duties and determined which of us would carry out what assignments to pull it all together. With zero room for error, I decided I better lean into my strengths of administration and organization and allow Sarah to attend to the more "spiritual" side of things because I felt she was much more gifted than I was in those areas.

In between my seminary class assignments, church assignments, and family obligations, I diligently went about completing my tasks. Then I received the text. Sarah was no longer going to be able to participate in the planning or execution of this event. It was a terrible blow. The retreat was only a couple of months away. It was bad enough that she was telling me that she would not be attending and I would be running the retreat by myself, but she also had not completed the tasks she had agreed to do to date. JILTED! I panicked because not only did I need to figure out how to get everything done in short order, but I was also depending on her to make sure the retreat was a wonderful *spiritual* experience for the women. But just like that, I had been jilted and thrown into the deep end of the pool. Eventually, I pulled myself together, and with much prayer, the ministry and I moved forward and the retreat was wonderful. However, the whole endeavor personally cost me money, some sleepless nights, and many tears.

But the worst part was she never told me why. Sarah walked away from the ministry and soon after, the church. And to this day, I do not know why. I felt abandoned, rejected, forgotten, and forsaken. I felt jilted.

Trying to recover from the trauma and expense of the previous year, we planned the events for our Women's Weekend to be held at the church the next year. With a new and faithful assistant servant leader and co-laborer in place, we went about the task of gathering a committee to make sure we dotted all our i's and crossed all of our t's. The women were excited. We had a breakfast planned for Saturday and two dynamic preachers to bless us on Sunday. Everything was going fabulously. Then on the Friday of our weekend, I received a call from Anita, one of our guest preachers. She was not going to be able to make it on Sunday. JILTED AGAIN! We talked and *I* prayed with *her*. Though I understood the reason she chose not to come, I could not believe this was happening again. I needed to find a replacement and fast!

I became panicked and anxious all over again. The prior year's retreat involved planning, coordinating, and directing—areas where I felt comfortable in my gifting. But now I was going to have to step in for *the preacher* with little more than 48 hours' notice. I needed the Lord to see my plight and move in an extraordinary and supernatural way. And that is exactly what He did! Not only did The Lord give me a Word for the people, but 20 souls joined church that Sunday (many of them candidates for baptism)! I was so grateful to be used in His service in such a powerful way. I was also very grateful for the sweet communion I experienced during those 48 hours when He ministered directly to my heart. Hallelujah!

Dear Diary, Fast-forward, I find myself here again. We have prayed and planned for another year's Women's Weekend to leave the women encouraged and edified and for God to be glorified. But today is Thursday and I just got word that our preacher for Sunday is unable to make it. She is ill and hospitalized and her inability to come is not of her own doing at all. *Is it okay to say I am starting to feel like I am being jilted by God Himself?*

Okay, I was in my feelings and being a little dramatic. Of course, I have not been jilted by God. He is **always** true to His Word:

> He will never leave you nor forsake you—Deuteronomy 31:6 (NIV)

> I can do all this through him who gives me strength—Philippians 4:13 (NIV)

> With man this is impossible, but with God all things are possible—Matthew 19:26 (NIV)

Not only have I read (and taught) these words, but they are also imprinted on my heart as God has shown me His favor over and over and over again. As I reflect back on each of these incidents, I see the hand of the Lord at work for me and in me.

Sarah had become a crutch to me. I depended on her "spirituality" to be in touch with the move of the Holy Spirit. To know how to pray and to discern who to use where. I am clear that despite whatever her reasons were, God moved her out of the way so that the "Spirit" I would depend on would be His. I said I had faith and I professed that I trusted Him but a faith untested is a faith unsure. James 1:2-8 reminds us that various testing and trials are designed to help us grow. God used the feelings of abandonment I was experiencing to draw me closer to Himself, and He reminded me that the "success" of a thing is defined by dependence on Him. In fact, the theme that I had selected for that very retreat was *Rejoice!*

1 Thessalonians 5:16-18 NKJV

[16] Rejoice always, [17] pray without ceasing, [18] in everything give thanks; for this is the will of God in Christ Jesus for you.

Duh.

I love Anita dearly, and she has often expressed her regret for not being able to join us that following year. I have assured her that I hold no ill will. I am so clear that everything, even the short notice, was a move of God. I had selected her to be the last preacher of the weekend because I thought she would be the showstopper. God made it so I would remember that *He* is the showstopper! One plants, one waters, but only God gives the increase, and through the weakness of preaching, He showed Himself mighty that Sunday morning when I stood and delivered the message, He gave to me that Sunday morning. And once again, He has seen fit to give me what I needed just when I needed it. I delivered the Word of God. It was well received by the congregation, and more importantly, I heard a "well done, daughter" in my Spirit.

So, no, God has not jilted me at all. People may come and go. They may disappoint, and sometimes they even disappear. Conversely, God continually demonstrates His grace and wisdom, majesty and power, working all things for the good for those who love Him and are called according to His purpose as He said He would. I am continuously in awe of Him and reminded of my need to fully depend on Him.

Jilted Summary
Christine O. James

A Closing Point of View:

Pastors' wives are a hard-working group of people. Beautiful women who are precious to God. We show up in partnership with our husbands, seeking to offer our very best to be a blessing to God's people and the surrounding community. More often than not this group of unpaid skilled workers generously serve wherever the pastor finds that there is a need. Familial feelings develop as we serve alongside the members that our husbands shepherd. We lead them, love them and share our very lives with them. We check on them when they're sick, sit with them in the loss of a loved one, yet we have no control over when or how they leave. It's a very unnatural relationship. Church is one of the few places where people just disappear. They just stop showing up and we have no idea why.

When people leave, we grieve. Our minds are filled with questions about what we may have done or said to cause them to leave. We care, so we find ourselves wondering if they are sick or injured. We ask other people, "Have you seen or heard from brother or sister so and so?" I have found myself perplexed with thoughts about "Why?" "Why was it so easy for them to detach after all that we have done and been through together? Why didn't they come talk to us, even if only to say goodbye?" I may never know the answers to those questions. But those questions become secondary as I reflect on the life and ministry of Jesus. He fed thousands, healed many more. He taught people, cared for people, even showed them his power to raise a person from the dead. Yet, at the foot of the cross, during the hour when he was most alone, there were three women and a young disciple nearby. How lonely is that!?! He even felt forsaken by the Father. He knew his mission but felt sadly alone.

I am personally very grateful that Jesus did not come off that cross. He stayed there for you and for me. We do this work because Jesus trusts us to model his love to his people. In the midst of disappointment, heartbreak and any uncertainty about people, we serve excellently as unto the Lord. Our love wanes, but His love is unfailing toward us and the people we serve.

Scriptures for Prayerful Reflection:

> Because of the Lord's great love we are not consumed, for his compassions never fail. They are new every morning;
>
> great is your faithfulness. I say to myself, "The Lord is my portion; therefore I will wait for him."
>
> ~ Lamentations 3:22-24 NIV

> "Can a mother forget the baby at her breast and have no compassion on the child she has borne? Though she may forget, I will not forget you! See, I have engraved you on the palms of my hands; your walls are ever before me.
>
> ~ Isaiah 49:15-16 NIV

> As you come to him, the living Stone—rejected by humans but chosen by God and precious to him—you also, like living stones, are being built into a spiritual house to be a holy priesthood, offering spiritual sacrifices acceptable to God through Jesus Christ.
>
> ~ 1 Peter 2:4-5 NIV

Let's Pray Together:

Lord, how grateful I am that you are a God who hears and answers prayer. Your Word tells us that before a word was on our tongue, you answered. God, thank you for the sacrifice you gave in your son Jesus who knows all about the temptations and pain we feel. When we are tempted to quit and throw in the towel, to believe that our labor has been in vain, please remind us of our hope in you. Holy Spirit, lead us into the truth that God's love never fails. Help us to remember that the seed we sow unto you will indeed produce fruit. Although we may not see it, help us to rest in your truth that as we sow, we shall reap. Protect our hearts, and protect our minds as we walk with you, seeking to do all that you have assigned us to do. We love you Oh God because you first loved us.

In Jesus' name, we pray, Amen.

JEALOUSY
Contributors

Introduction

Dr. Larry L. Anderson Jr.

What About Me?!?

Christine O. James

A Journey To Surrender

Cissy McNickle

Ride or Die Girl

Kimberly A. Anderson

Jealousy Summary

Christine O. James

Introduction
Dr. Larry L Anderson Jr.

I've been pastoring for twenty years, and every two to three years during my ministry, there seems to be a woman who seems to have more interest in me than they have in God. This is based on my wife's observation and perspective. There is always this woman whose motives or intentions she questions. This person's attire, participation, and personality all come into question. I would get extremely frustrated during these seasons, as I have never had an affair or been inappropriate with a woman during our marriage. And no woman in twenty years has ever said or done anything overtly in my presence to suggest they wanted to have a relationship with me beyond my shepherding of them. Now, this is not to say no woman has thought, imagined, or even wanted to have a relationship with me beyond pastoring. I'm only stating that none of them have ever made moves on me to go in that direction. I used the word "overtly" earlier intentionally because a few trusted individuals have warned me of women in the church who seem to have eyes for me. I have also sensed a spiritual uncomfortableness with certain women over the years, which I intentionally chose to avoid.

I have been honest with myself and God concerning physical attraction, and I also have an accountability partner in my assistant pastor, Dr. D.

Kyle Canty. If there was anyone I found or I believe may have found me attractive, he and I would put up barriers to minimize that contact. Just being honest about it to God helps remove the desire and telling someone else about it removes the secrecy, which always adds to the temptation. I have never met with women alone, and I have employed this practice throughout my entire ministry. I have also shared with my wife that she does not now or ever have a reason to be jealous because I am not going to violate my relationship with the Lord by having an affair. So, with all that being said, there is no reason in the world for my wife to ever feel insecure or jealous, right? Wrong.

As I began to pray about this as a chapter for this book, the Lord flipped the script and made me imagine my wife and I serving in reverse roles. Now, for those of you who cannot imagine a woman being a pastor, bear with me for illustration purposes. I was led to envision her as the pastor, with seventy-five percent of the church being men. Men who waited to hug her following every Sunday service. Men who had her cell number and were able to text or contact her when they needed a word from their pastor. Men who seem to really admire her and desire her attention and affirmation consistently. I began to wonder how I would handle this. Would I stare at them to show that my North Philly upbringing was still in me and they better recognize? Would I make sure I held her hand, hugged her, or kissed her during service each week to mark my territory? I wondered exactly how I would handle my wife being the center of attention day after day, week after week, and year after year. Well, what the Holy Spirit so painfully convicted me of concerning jealousy was that I would have never handled it anywhere close to the way my wife has handled it over these last two decades.

I had to ask myself, "If she felt uncomfortable about a woman at church and she is sharing that concern with me, why am I so uncomfortable with hearing that?" Well, it's because I want her to love and accept everyone. It's because I don't want any drama at church. And I want her to just trust me, so regardless of what another woman's thoughts or intentions might be, I want her to feel secure that I'm not going to allow anything to come between us. However, even with me feeling the exact same trust in her, I still would have a problem being in the presence of men who had some attraction for my wife, and I would definitely voice it to her and probably immaturely demonstrate it to them.

I wish I could say my conviction over jealousy ended with the women's issue, but I have also accused my wife of being jealous of the ministry. God has called and equipped me to serve in the church and in the world. I am a Kingdom-focused individual, meaning I try to make an impact for God's glory with my life in every sphere that I enter. This is one of the reasons why I have been co-vocational my entire ministry, meaning I intentionally work additional jobs beyond pastoring.

I have literally asked my wife the question, "Would you like me to serve God or you?" This was an attempt to help her recognize her selfishness in trying to compete with God. However, the Holy Spirit interrupted my self-righteousness and forced me to remember that serving my wife was also honoring God. Indeed, the Holy Spirit had convicted me of my important self-worth to the Kingdom by reminding me of 1 Timothy 3:5 and my first ministry being my home.

As crazy as this may sound to you, I want you to hear me when I say this: I love working. I love thinking, praying, and strategizing ways to get people to know and fall in love with Jesus. I don't love preaching; I don't love being at church or having church meetings. But I am truly at peace sharing my faith, sharing the Bible in life-transformative ways, and sitting with a computer in my lap twenty-four hours a day, thinking of ways to help other pastors and churches make an impact for God's glory. Vacation and relaxation for me is reading a book or writing a book that will help me do those things I just shared.

My wife, on the other hand, sees my phone, my computer, and the church not as extensions of my love for the Lord but as her competition for my love and attention. My wife did not marry a pastor; she married the CEO of a record label. She watched my life spiritually transform and witnessed me resign from the world to follow Christ. She supported me while I went back to school for ten years to get a BS. in Bible and my MDiv and DMin degrees. She supported me as I was licensed, ordained, and installed as a pastor. And over nineteen years she has had to share me with hundreds of people who would come to call me Pastor. People whom I admittedly felt called to cater to and whose needs I believed I had to always place above my own and mistakenly even above my family. I prayed for and with the members, I taught them, I visited them and I was basically on call to them 24-7 to earn their love and support all the while taking my wife's love and support for granted. To be honest and transparent, my wife was not jealous of the church, the ministry, or God. She was only voicing her feelings of neglect by her husband, whom she had every right to want to spend time with. As an introvert, I prefer to be alone as much as possible, and engaging with people really drains me. However, my whole life is based on functioning as an extension of Christ, and therefore, as much as it may exhaust me, I still was committed to giving all I had to serve. Unfortunately, when I returned home from church, I sadly would come inside the house not wanting any more human contact, and unfortunately, the person who loved me most and was always waiting on me to love her got slighted.

I've grown over the years, and I came to realize that in order to have a healthy life and some balance between my family and my ministry, I needed to make some substantial changes. I had to ordain deacons, created a pastoral staff and a leadership team, and equipped and empowered them to share the ministry load. I recognized and elevated a rotation of preachers who now preach strategically to bless the body and to ensure I have quality time to spend with my wife. My wife and I are dating now like never before and are able to enjoy some weekends without sermon prep. I have a leadership team to wrestle with our church's vision and goals while strategizing to achieve them. I have small groups that are the first line of support for those members in the hospital or in immediate need. Coincidentally, I have learned to say no to various opportunities as well. I have limited my outside speaking engagements. I have even cut down on some of the volunteer organizations I serve.

Listen, everything I was doing was great. They were all worthwhile organizations whose mission it was to save the world, both spiritually and socioeconomically. However, my Savior did not call me to save the world; that's what He died for. I took time to examine my life and ask myself what was most important and what God was truly calling me to. I had to examine my motives for even saying yes to so many things and to so many people. I never saw myself as a people pleaser, but somehow, I discovered my saying yes was designed to make sure that I was liked, needed, and even wanted. In addition, somehow, I believe I was unconsciously trying to pay God back for all He had done for me.

Finally, I must say that it was my meditation on Exodus 34:14 and Ephesians 5:22-24 that reminded me that God is a jealous God. In fact, He says my name is jealous. In addition, I was reminded that the body of Christ is Jesus' bride and not mine. Due to this revelation, I have been trying my best not to embrace the church or any other non-profit as my mistress. I'm not claiming now to be perfect and have a perfect balance of life and ministry, but I am acknowledging that I am a recovering workaholic and by God's grace I will stay in recovery.

What About Me?!?
Christine O. James

Dear Diary, Creative discipleship is one of my husband's strongest gifts. He knows how to connect with people in a way that is refreshing to them. I had no idea how that same gift would become a point of jealousy in my life. Slot racing cars in the winter, bike riding in the spring and summer. This was how my husband connected with some of the male leadership of our first pastorate. One would think that I, his wife, would feel good about the bonds he was building with the men he was discipling, and I did until it became my competitor, or so I felt. When I was home doing laundry, waiting to be relieved by Daddy, I would get a call saying, "I'll be there in a few…" Who knew that a few would be an hour or two?

I would attempt to put on a facade of being laissez-faire about his time out, but the truth is, I was jealous that he got to be out, away from it all. Away from screaming, fighting children, away from the constant requests for one more thing, a cookie, a movie, or "Can you take us here or there?" The household burdens of laundry, cooking and the dishes that followed. I was overwhelmed. I wanted to go out to play and connect with adult humans too. Despite my attempts at having a "spiritual" and generous attitude about it all, I could feel the slow burn begin to rise up in me. Instead of placing laundry into the washer, I'd begin throwing it in, grumbling throughout the entire process.

Sensing my anger and disappointment when he arrived home, my husband, you know, the creative one, decided to take a different approach in talking the situation out. He picked up the camcorder and took on the role of reporter and began to interview me. He posed as an unbiased reporter seeking to get to the bottom of the issue. His opening comment, "You seem very angry with your husband..." Can you just imagine how infuriated I felt as I rolled my eyes in response to his question. I continued folding laundry and placing it in each individual's basket in an exaggerated fashion. I didn't care that I was being recorded. Then he asked, "Do you feel like your husband doesn't care?" Oh no, I could feel his empathy start to come through. I didn't want to feel it. I wanted to stay in the state I was in, a mad, disappointed martyr. I wanted to yell, "Don't try to be sweet now! You don't care about me!" The truth is, I didn't feel like anyone cared, and I especially wondered if God cared.

To everything there is a season, and during that season, I felt forgotten. Prior to marriage, I had earned two degrees and had a rather promising career. I was a manager in charge of people and systems. People listened to me and cared about what I had to say about things. But now, I was at home, doing what felt like mundane things at the time. Endless diaper changes, countless peanut butter and jelly sandwiches, along with endless whining and complaining. My frequent cry to God would be, "What about me? Don't I get to have a life too?" I remember even asking God the question, "Do you like men better than you like women?" I didn't want to face the fact that this was my life for this season.

As I look back into some of my old journals, so much of my writing was written from points of despair and disappointment. It's kind of embarrassing that I rarely chronicled the moments of joy or even times of contentment. I left out the milestones of achievements made in our homeschool process, the vacations that we were able to take and make good memories together because our children were learning at home. I didn't write about the times when my husband would work from home so that he could facilitate our children's schooling while I did consultant work outside of the home. And how could I leave out the years when my husband released me to care for my dying mother? When I arrived home after taking care of a terminally ill beloved mother, he continually made sure that the children gave me space to be alone, to be quiet and grieve. Jealousy can really cloud reality. Maybe instead of being called the "green-eyed" monster, jealousy should be called the "cloudy-eyed" monster. Jealousy tricks you into believing that the difficult moments will always be there. It makes you fight for rights that have already been given.

Even now, I find that I have to check myself at times so that I don't start trying to evaluate what is "fair" or not. Comparison with my husband or other people and circumstances robs me of seeing God correctly. It robs me of the joy that comes from being in His presence. In His presence I can evaluate my life with proper perspective. Like the fact that difficulties and trials produce deeper, more genuine faith. When I compare myself to others and operate in jealousy, I can run the risk of missing the good things in front of me. Anyone who knows me well knows that my husband and my children are the greatest joys of my life. They are all truly gifts from God. But the important thing that is often missed as people see us flourishing as a family today is that all of the beauty, gifts, talents and togetherness were born of seed sown in some very rocky soil. Those arid, dry places were all a part of God's plan to train us and build us up according to His divine plan. His plan is that we would love Him more than anything. Those times of sowing in tears and disappointment have reaped a harvest of blessings.

One of his final questions during his mock interview all of those years ago was this, "Do you believe that God knows that your husband is a pastor and that you have three small children and baskets full of laundry?" That was the question that put the nail in my angry coffin. My husband knew that I loved God. He knew that I knew and had evidence that God loved me despite my current angry state. He knew that I couldn't deny God's grace, which was and is sufficient. I couldn't deny his love and provision for me. So, he asked me the question, "Do you believe?" Isn't that always the question? It's always a question of faith. I wanted what I wanted from my husband while discounting what God was and is continually offering to me. Because my husband was right in front of me, it was easy to make demands of him and punish him with my anger when the demand was not met.

As I further ponder this issue of jealousy, in my life and yours, I wonder what would happen in our hearts if we really believed that God is good. What would happen if we really believed that he would withhold no good thing from us? The prayer and hope I have is that jealousy would be replaced by anticipation. Anticipation of good gifts from a good God, not from man.

A Journey To Surrender
Cissy McNickle

Dear Diary, I am a leader. I was born this way. I am the oldest of three children and can remember, at a young age, feeling the pull to organize, direct, and lead when there was no one else doing it. Thinking back on it now, I never wanted to "run" for a leadership position. I never ran for class president or ANY school council position, but if there was a group project at school or later in life at work and no one took the lead, I couldn't help it; eventually, I would start leading.

In ministry, this quality worked well for me. I started serving as a young teenager in the children's ministry at my church and haven't stopped since. Leading in the church was a natural fit for me. Growing up I remember that I knew I would always serve in the church and felt a call to ministry when I was in high school. However, marrying a pastor was NEVER part of the plan. Later in life, I learned of Christian women who feel *called* to be a *pastor's wife*. Some even go to a Christian college and seminary to find and marry a pastor. Not me!

I went to a secular college and worked as an assistant youth leader during that time. Later I became the youth leader. I loved my job, and I loved my church. It wasn't until I was 28 that I met my future husband.

We became friends and served together on a week-long mission trip in Mexico. On the flight home, he asked me out on a date. I guess looking back it makes sense, but at the time I was overwhelmed at the thought of dating and potentially marrying a pastor. Not a boy in seminary learning his trade, but a man who had been serving in full-time ministry for over 15 years. I say this because my husband and I married later in life. We came into this relationship as fully functioning, *independent* adults, and this realization would become important for me to understand when I struggled to shift into the beautiful and challenging role of wife.

For the most part, the beginning was easy. Right after marriage, he was hired at a Christian college and life was fun! We worked with athletes and international kids. We were partners in crime. I found areas that I could serve and lead, and side-by-side, together, we led. A few years went by, and like many couples, we had kids. The beginning of becoming a mother has its own challenges, but I was at home with the babies (leading), he was at church (leading), and it worked. It wasn't until the kids got older that I realized the domain where I led felt infringed upon. And I did not adjust well!

The babies (three of them) are now kids, and Dad's involvement is naturally expected to increase. In my mind, this is great! We are entering a new phase of parenting and a new phase of our marriage. In reality, my husband and I are not always in agreement about the direction our parenting should go, but this is *my* territory! I am the mother! I lead at home! I wish I could say that I immediately and obediently *surrendered* my will to God and my husband, but I did not! I am a natural leader! *I've* got this!

Needless to say, the next several years of parenting were difficult. My husband and I were rarely on the same parenting page and at times I didn't think we were in the same book! And we have one child who loves to exploit this fact in our relationship! But I refused to give up or give in. One day in complete desperation, alone, on my way to church,

I sobbed out to God that I was so tired and frustrated. That I was "tired of being on different pages with my husband. Why can't we just get on the same page!!!!" And in my heart, in the quiet voice that God often uses to speak into my chaos, He said, "You can. You can get on the same page." I was so confused on how? I told God, "My husband will NEVER get on my page!" And God said, "No, but you can get on his page." What!? I almost wrecked the car in my shock! *I was right!* My husband was wrong. How do you relinquish leadership when you know you were meant to lead!? And then God asked, "Do you trust *me*? Do you trust that *I* can lead this family through the leadership of your *husband*? Do you trust that I can do that?" Can I put into action all that I say I believe about God? Is my faith just what I profess or is it more than that? Can I trust HIM to lead a flawed man as he leads our family? (I do recognize the irony in that.)

The questions in my mental dialogue continued. Can I set aside my pride and surrender? Can I lay down the role I *want* to have in my family and pick up the role God has *ordained* for me in my family? Ouch! I can recognize now that JEALOUSY had reared its ugly head. I was jealous of the role my husband was called to play. I saw his role as greater than the role I was called to fill. As a leader, yielding to the will of another has never been easy for me. *I* wanted the power to make the decisions for our family as I saw fit. *I* wanted to be the leader. *I* wanted control!! I don't know about anyone else, but for me, it seems to always come back to control! At the end of the day, my jealousy was the real issue at hand. It really had nothing to do with my husband, what he was called to do, and what I was called to do; it had EVERYTHING to do with pride, surrender, and control. And then God reminded me of His original question, "Do you trust me?" All of the turmoil and tears zeroed in on this one question, "DO I TRUST GOD?" Well, did I?

My answer to that question has been a work in progress every day since then. The answer is yes!!! A resounding yes!!! The process is proving to be more challenging. BUT I have seen my husband rise to the occasion.

He has led us through difficult crossroads with solutions that I never even saw. God has given me peace as I continue to lay down the pressure that comes with all questions being mine alone to answer and all solutions being mine alone to find.

I have also learned that ALL great leaders are also great followers! I am encouraged by Paul, the leader of the Gentile church, who said, "Follow me as I follow Christ" (1 Corinthians 11:1 MEV). I have not done this well, and MANY days I still flip the book back to my page, but each day I can choose to willfully and disobediently lead my family in my strength OR I can yield to God's leadership in my life and my family's life. I can choose to focus on what is *not* my role and be *jealous* of my husband OR I can *joyfully* follow my husband as he follows Christ.

Ride or Die Girl
Kim Anderson

Dear Diary, I keep asking myself what happened. Is there something wrong with me? I thought having God in our lives would make our lives so much better, but instead, I find myself feeling like I have no control over my life, and I'm wondering if I'm called to sacrifice my husband because he is willing to sacrifice me, our children and everything and everyone else for the Lord. It's 2009 and it seems like I've been a single parent for the last ten years, and I honestly cannot take it anymore. But this is not the way it's always been. I married my best friend in 1997. He was not interested in pastoring then, nor was he even going to church when we got together. He always called me his "Ride or Die Girl" because I was willing to support him in any way he needed. Ironically, I'm the one who convinced him to go back to church. I even insisted that we get pre-marital counseling and get married in a church. The funny thing is, I was not even going to church myself at that time, but I knew it was the right thing to do, and so I wanted to do things the right way. It's amazing how my husband was the CEO of a rap record label and there were many groupies hanging around. There were half-naked girls on stage with his artist, and he would go on tour with the group, but I was never jealous or insecure during those days. However, the one that

I became jealous of more than any other was the church and how she stole my husband from me.

My husband's reluctance in going to church back then was about his self-imposed discipline and his commitment to always giving whatever he was involved in 110 percent. He shared with me that he was not attending church, not because he was an unbeliever but the exact opposite. He shared he had grown up in church, and he knew the Lord, and in fact, he believed in God so much that he could not be a hypocrite and go to church and continue to live the way he was currently living. He even shared that he felt he had a calling on his life. Well, let me say when he shared this information with me, I felt, of all the excuses a man could come up with for not attending church, this had to be the absolute best. He had the nerve to want me to believe that he actually loved God too much to go to church. Wow!

As my husband began to give in and attend church with me, I started to see a change in Him. That commitment and that desire to give his all began to surface. He and I were saved, and we rededicated our lives to the Lord shortly following. The world and the life we once knew were being transformed to reflect our new knowledge and relationship with the Lord. I was excited about this development in our lives. I was his "Ride or Die Girl" and I felt God would surely make both of us better individually and collectively, bringing us closer to Him and one another. Because we had young children at home who needed attention, I was left at home while he attended the Wednesday evening Bible studies and the Saturday morning evangelism outreach. He was always an avid reader, so he eagerly began reading the Bible from beginning to end. I was excited that he was so committed to growing in the Word, but I did not realize he was also growing away from me. I, being a mommy and wife, did not have the luxury to stop all that I was doing and mirror his pursuit of the Lord. But I did not complain because I was his "Ride or Die Girl."

As his hunger for the Lord increased, he resigned from the record label, and his commitment to serving at the church also increased. If the doors to the church were open, he just had to be there. He also decided to go to Bible college, followed by seminary to obtain his master's and doctorate degrees. I understood and supported his decision to go back to school, but I did not know this decision would mean he would be out of the home all of the time. His absence also didn't allow us to grow spiritually together as I would have liked. I feel this somewhat hindered my journey in the beginning. I worked full-time, came home and became the wife and mother my family needed. I knew that being a stay-at-home wife was not an option. My employment provided good medical and health care benefits, which were necessary for our quality of life. I had good credit and was able to help secure us a home. Although he was not where I was financially at that time, and he was missing in action physically, it was still all good because I was his "Ride or Die Girl."

God came first, and I wanted to be a good wife, so I tried not to complain about him always being unavailable, but I wondered, "At what point is this situation just unfair?" I wondered, "When do I get a break from handling everything in our home with our kids, with our bills?" Every decision seems like it was mine to make if it did not involve the Bible or church. I was feeling so alone, and I felt left behind in so many ways. I also felt guilty for wanting to spend time with my husband. Navigating life as a pastor's wife posed significant challenges, particularly in these initial stages. This was all too new to me. I often felt isolated, struggling to express my true self. Balancing trust in God with personal struggles became a delicate challenge. My husband was on fire for the Lord, which was great, but I felt left behind. I was just exhausted. I was jealous of his life and everyone else around me. Having fun with my husband seemed to have gotten lost. And even when he was home, he was not really present with us. Sadly, I knew if he had a choice between me, our children, or the church, the church would win out every time. Neither my husband nor I had ever served in church as adults. We also had not been in church, at this level, long enough to see a healthy pastor and wife relationship play out in front of us. When my husband became the pastor during his third year of his master's program, we both thought it came sooner than we expected or wanted. However, we were faithful and committed to whatever God wanted, so we said yes. The work-life balance wasn't working. Looking back, I believe my perspectives weren't fully shared and valued, and I sometimes still feel this way after 19 years.

My husband had a pastor and a mentor to help him grow into the position, but I had no one. As the pastor of our church decided to step down due to marital issues, his wife was not in a position to help me. I was not an avid reader like my husband, so I had not read the Bible from beginning to end. I did not feel called or equipped to lead a women's ministry. I do not play the organ or sing. Therefore, I was wondering where I fit in the church and what I was called to do. I was told loving and supporting my husband was my calling, and so once again, I'm called to stand by him and let him be all that God has called him to be. In other words, continue being his "Ride or Die Girl."

I remember listening to my husband preach one Sunday morning and he said some words I will never forget. He said, "Your wife and your family are your first ministry." My mouth dropped wide open and my eyes welled up because I admittedly had never heard that said before and definitely not by him. I could not wait to get home to question this new revelation he uttered out of his mouth. I shared with him that not only do I feel like I don't come first, but that I don't know where I or the kids fit in his life or his ministry. I shared my disdain for his phone and how it was glued to his hand and how we could not have dinner without being interrupted by someone from church. I shared how he would always miss family events because of ministry, and it seemed we no longer had a life outside of the church. I shared how I missed him being my best friend and how the quality time we used to spend together no longer existed. I shared how I loved being his "Ride or Die Girl," but it feels more like dying instead of riding together anywhere.

We cried together and he repented and apologized. I wanted to go to counseling, but I believe he was too embarrassed at that time to allow someone to know how he had become the very thing he avoided—resisting the Lord many years before because he didn't want to be seen as a hypocrite. Not because of some sin or doing anything to violate his character but by allowing the church to become his idol and allowing the members' likes to replace his family's love

Fast-forward to 2024, I can say things have changed dramatically. He has not missed a kid's game, a daddy-daughter dance, or our date night in the last ten years. He has learned to say no to the church and to opportunities that he once felt he had to say yes to. He has empowered the church staff and ministers to step in and step up and be who God has called them to be instead of thinking he has to play the role of God in the church. Yes, he is still busy but vacation is a part of our normal lives. Yes, he still has that phone but he texts instead of talking, so I am no longer being asked to be silent as he has learned how to silence that phone. And yes, we have discussed and look forward to retiring and moving and spending even more quality time together as I believe he wants to spend time with me just as much as I want to spend time with him. I love my husband-pastor, and I am at a place where I understand the calling we have on our lives. This calling is by all means a sacrifice, as every member who calls him pastor truly believes he needs to be there when they need him most. However, I know where he will be as he has learned his first ministry is with his "Ride or Die Girl."

Jealousy Summary
Christine O. James

A Closing Point of View:

Jealousy is an insidious creature. Often called the green-eyed monster, I think it shows up in many colors in varied circumstances. When we think of jealousy, it's often thought about in relation to people and one person being chosen over another. However, in pastoral ministry, the other woman can manifest in the form of an organization, the church. Because we are serving the Lord, we want to do it with excellence, but sometimes excellence can be confused with perfectionism and overwork.

There is an imbalance that can occur between the ministry in the home and the ministry outside of the home. This sort of juggling act can sometimes pit us against each other when, in reality, we are all doing the best we can to do and be all that God has called us to be. I know that there are indeed times when jealousy is the result of evil intentions from human encounters, but more often than not, jealousy signals a need for deeper, honest and open communication between the two parties involved. We must be careful not to fall into the idolatry of human individuals. Making demands on people and or comparing ourselves to our husbands or others completely underestimates the sovereign power of God and what he wants to do in our lives.

Each congregational ministry has its unique components and challenges that don't come with a set of blueprints for navigation. It is challenging for both the pastor and wife to walk this out while building and shepherding a family. There are far too few mentors who are willing to share wisdom about how to navigate the ministry and family life. And if they do share, they are usually shared from a behavioral perspective, like "how to be a good pastor's wife," but rarely from the realm of practical empathy and encouragement to move forward. Too often we find ourselves both traveling on parallel paths, heading toward a similar goal, but missing each other's hearts. Perhaps grace is the answer, trusting that God sees and has a perfect plan for us all.

Scriptures for Prayerful Reflection:

> Humble yourselves, therefore, under God's mighty hand, that he may lift you up in due time. Cast all your anxiety on him because he cares for you. Be alert and of sober mind. Your enemy the devil prowls around like a roaring lion looking for someone to devour.
>
> ~ 1 Peter 5:6-8 NIV

> Yes, my soul, find rest in God; my hope comes from him. Truly he is my rock and my salvation; he is my fortress; I will not be shaken. My salvation and my honor depend on God; he is my mighty rock, my refuge. Trust in him at all times, you people; pour out your hearts to him, for God is our refuge.
>
> ~ Psalm 62:5-8 NIV

> Who is wise and understanding among you? Let them show it by their good life, by deeds done in the humility that comes from wisdom. But if you harbor bitter envy and selfish ambition in your

hearts, do not boast about it or deny the truth. Such "wisdom" does not come down from heaven but is earthly, unspiritual, demonic. For where you have envy and selfish ambition, there you find disorder and every evil practice.

~ James 3:13-16 NIV

Let's Pray Together:

Lord God, we thank you for the people you have allowed us to walk alongside in this thing called life. We thank you for spouses, for friendships, for project partnerships. It was you who decided that man should not be alone, so we thank you for togetherness. Help us O God to not make more of people than we make of you. You are the God who is more than enough. You, God, supply all of our needs according to your riches in glory and for that we say thank you. Help us to keep a proper perspective about our human relationships. Help us to remember that you alone are God. We reject all forms of idolatry and place you alone on the throne of our hearts. In Jesus' name, Amen.

JUDAS
Contributors

Introduction
Dr. Larry L. Anderson Jr.

In the Face of Betrayal
Christine O. James

The Risk of Trusting
Cynthia Hawthorne Armstrong

Judas Among Us
Shirley A. Wilson

Judas Summary
Christine O. James

Introduction
Dr. Larry L Anderson Jr.

When you think of Judas, you think of the betrayal of a person who was a disciple of Jesus for years. He was in Jesus' inner circle of ministry. He was someone you thought was a faithful follower and supporter all the way up to the point when he wasn't any longer. However, we read the gospel in hindsight, with the knowledge of who Judas is and what he's going to do, so it's easy not to get too attached to his character because you know betrayal is coming. But yet it still hurts to see Peter's cursing and denial of Christ when persecution was on the line, or Thomas's doubt concerning Jesus' resurrection after years of them doing ministry together, as these moments feel much like betrayal. See, in the body of Christ, betrayal is not often experienced by the person you hate, stabbing you in the back, but rather by someone with the sinful spirit of Judas, who you thought was faithful, only to betray you after years of friendship. Below are two out of hundreds of encounters I've experienced over the last couple of decades.

Judas (not their real name) was young and charismatic and so excited about the gospel. They had a contagious energy and a selfless work ethic that made me excited to give them opportunities to serve. I was willing to pour all I had into them because I truly thought I was making an investment in them and the future of the ministry. Of course, Judas had their battles with sin but what new and young believer doesn't? Therefore, I exercised grace, offered correction for their behavior, and continued to instruct and disciple them because I truly believed Judas was on Jesus' team. I believed that the more time I spent with them and the more I opened up to them, the more faithful they would become and the more they would come to realize and appreciate the investment I was sacrificially pouring into them. However, there were others in the church who were questioning the rationale behind the personal investment being made into Judas. There were members who would have killed to have a portion of the time I was spending with Judas. But I dismissed these members' complaints as jealousy, and I reasoned these concerns away because of the working chemistry instantly fostered with Judas and me. But just as quickly as Judas accepted the truth of the Gospel, Judas rejected that same truth for the lust of the eyes. Judas' charisma turned out to be a con. Judas had gotten involved in so many sinful twists and turns it made my head spin.

Upon further investigation, I came to realize that the behavior Judas was participating in within the church was the same behavior they demonstrated in the world. I was so embarrassed and felt so betrayed by Judas, yet I was still willing to help them repent and walk out a process of restoration. However, Judas continued to deny their involvement in all of the alleged behavior and continued to look me in the face and lie. It was like the biblical kiss of Judas being played out in real-time. Our Judas left the church almost as quickly as they came, as well as the Christian faith altogether, for that matter. A few years later Judas contacted me to apologize for their behavior, but that pain of betrayal will never be forgotten. I'm not sure if Judas ever truly accepted Christ as their Savior, as I have come to discover saying the sinners' prayer and getting into that baptism pool is not evidence of salvation; it just makes you a part of the church crew, just like the Judas of the Bible, was in Jesus' inner crew.

The next Judas we'll discuss was even smoother than the first. They had all the right moves and knew all the right things to say. Judas had come to the church as a guest with their fiancée, a member of our church, seeking marital counseling. Of course, I shared with them that I could not perform a wedding with an unequally yoked couple as their fiancée had made a public declaration of their salvation to the Lord many years ago. Judas presented no pushback to the biblical position on unequally yoked couples and communicated their desire to know the Lord, accept the Lord, and become one with their fiancée and their Lord. Therefore, we began premarital counseling sessions with the understanding that they would need to come to know and accept Christ as their Savior before a wedding could actually take place. So, counseling session after counseling session took place with all the laughter, compliance, and cooperation of the couple. Salvation was ultimately confessed and a baptism was conducted. Church attendance was better and even participation in non-Sunday events increased.

The wedding finally took place, and shockingly, Judas never stepped back into the church after they heard the words "I do." Initially, I did not think anything of it as both of them were immediately missing in action. Then months went by, and as I began to inquire, I was informed how Judas was struggling with their faith and was not interested in church anymore and they were questioning who God truly was. This was upsetting, as it was a total 180 from what they presented themselves to be prior to reciting their wedding nuptials. But what was even more upsetting was our longstanding members who professed their faith in Jesus so many years prior, disappearing without a trace as well, immediately following the nuptials. There was never a call, a text, or any type of communication shared with me of a struggle being had by them to totally walk away from the faith and the church. The lack of communication from my member was, in fact, so strange it made me wonder if the whole process of them getting their non-believing fiancée to attend church and submit to counseling was a setup prepared by them. I wondered if it was possible that my member was feeding the necessary dialogue to their non-believing fiancée just so they could make it to the wedding day, while both of them were in on the ultimate plan to walk away.

See, here's what being betrayed does to someone. It makes you question the motives behind everyone who's ever done you wrong. You wonder if what they had done to you was premeditated. You question if any part of your relationship with them was real. You question how you could be so naïve. You wonder why you didn't see it coming, or what you could have done differently. Ultimately, a part of your trust and your willingness to get close to someone is damaged. Your willingness to sacrifice your time for those risky people is shut down. You begin to distance yourself and create emotional barriers to protect yourself from being taken advantage of again. And then the Holy Spirit reminds you that Jesus washed Judas' feet knowing that he would betray Him. You're reminded that even Judas had a purpose in Christ's ministry. You're reminded of Luke 6:32-35 NIV, which says, "If you love those who love you, what credit is that to you? Even sinners love those who love them ... But love your enemies, do good to them, and lend to them without expecting to get anything back. Then your reward will be great, and you will be children of the Most High because he is kind to the ungrateful and wicked."

I share these experiences to show that no one is off-limits when it comes to the Judas experience. The pastor's wife has to have so much wisdom and discernment because anything they say or do can be used against them. If they have a moment of transparency at church and discuss a problem they might be having at home, it can instantly become a rumor about what's going wrong in the pastor's home. Therefore, the natural path most of these women take to avoid Judas is to isolate themselves from meaningful relationships and ministries within the church. To protect themselves and their families, they are forced to keep everyone at a distance. Unfortunately, this can make them seem unapproachable or snobbish, when, in fact, they are often starving for a true relationship. I know that as a pastor betrayal is an unfortunate part of the job. You must learn how to forgive and move on from it.

But let me pause to just speak to the pastors who are reading this right now. How are we as pastors preparing and protecting our wives from this type of hurt and betrayal? Are we expecting them to simply accept it as a part of their calling to be a pastor's wife? Do we expect them to develop hard hearts and emotional buttons that can be turned on and off to cope with betrayal, as many of us have done? Are we open to hearing about their painful betrayal experiences, or are we dismissive because we've been hurt so many times and we don't want to hear another story that can cause us pain? Pastors, the last thing our wives need after feeling betrayed at church is to feel betrayed at home by their husbands and pastors. We must love and shepherd our wives through their wounds. We must acknowledge and applaud them for having the courage to even take a risk on relationships. A risk that many pastors' wives have been burned by taking and are no longer willing to take. We must share with them that we, too, have been hurt and betrayed, and we're still struggling with how to love like Jesus when we've been betrayed by Judas.

In the Face of Betrayal
Christine O. James

Dear Diary, No one wakes up one morning and decides that they will play the role of "betrayer." Judas was a smart man who simply thought he had a better plan, as do many of the people who attend our churches. After undergoing a tremendous spiritual battle with long-time members of our first pastorate, my husband sought to build a new core of leaders who would help establish a church community guided by biblical principles and not by the traditions of men. This new plan included an intensive discipleship program that encouraged members to live their lives with a biblical worldview.

I was asked to facilitate a group of 8 women through a 12-week practical discussion about Christ being formed in our everyday lives. After about 3-4 weeks into our time together, I got the flu and had to turn the group over to my assistant. She was an older woman who had been a long-time member of the church. My husband wanted me to train in this new discipleship model of growing mature believers.

During my 2-week recuperation period, I would check in with my assistant leader to see how the group was going. She reported that things were going well and that I should take all of the time I needed to regain my health. When I returned the following week, I found out that I had essentially been voted off the "island." Each woman took turns around the circle to tell me things like, *"You're not fun! When you weren't here, we were rolling on the floor with laughter!"* I listened intently as the flaming arrows shot through my soul. All the while, I was amazed that I did not cry. I had a sort of out-of-body experience where I felt like I had been lifted out of the room. I had a fresh understanding of the Scripture, "Thou O Lord are a shield about me." I honestly felt like God had sent an Angelic guard to protect me as the insults and accusations continued to be hurled toward me.

When they all said their peace, I paused and listened, waiting for God to tell me what to say. I wanted to get up and run out of there screaming, "Never again! I will never open my heart to women again." Instead, these are the words that came out of my mouth, "I have heard all that you have said, and I understand that you all had a 'great time' with my assistant; however, the problem that you all must confront is that the pastor of the church you have chosen to be a member of has chosen me to be the discipleship leader of this group."

I closed the meeting with prayer and headed to the dining room of the home, where the after-meeting was held, to partake of refreshments. This time was intended to foster bonding through informal fellowship. I ate the food but tasted nothing. I was numb. I'm sure that I made polite conversation as I was trained by my mother to do, but I remember none of it.

Driving home was a blur to me. Again, I was so grateful for Angelic protection. When I arrived home, it was dark in the house. My young children were fast asleep. I thought my husband was too. I sat at my dining room table in the dark. Head in hands, I pondered what had taken place in the group, still amazed that no tears were shed. My husband, having heard me come in, came downstairs, saw my demeanor, and immediately asked what was wrong. I vaguely remember uttering the words, "I don't know." I was shell-shocked. The enemy had launched a scud missile designed to close my heart forever and keep me from a future serving God's people, especially women.

My husband's tenderness and compassion as he listened to me unfold the betrayal that happened in the meeting was a healing balm. It broke through the stupor and allowed me to see the enemy's venom for what it was. It was the familiar lie told to Eve way back in the Garden of Eden, "Hath God really said?" The attack on me was and sometimes still is, "Has God really called you to lead women?" What the enemy did not know was that betrayal set the stage for another level of maturity in how I walk with God and his people.

The story of the Last Supper, where Jesus sat with all of his disciples for a final meal, always encourages me in times like these. He knew that Judas was at the table; he knew what Judas was going to do. The father had prepared him, and I am so thankful that the father had also prepared me for the very disappointing betrayal. These were women that I loved, women with whom I had created fond memories and deep affection. I could not in a million years have imagined what they had planned for my return.

But God knew. Weeks before this meeting I was watching a jewelry commercial about an open-heart pendant for sale. The actress who was promoting the jewelry said something like this, "Momma always said, if you don't keep your heart open, nothing will be able to get in..." I felt very emotional watching the commercial because I knew that the Spirit of God was prompting me to pay attention. God knew that my heart had not healed from the battles and ongoing warfare of the previous pastorate where we served. These people were supposed to represent fresh hope. But instead, the enemy was using the folly of their humanity as a signal to me to never serve again in such a vulnerable capacity. I would often defend women when people would describe us as a fickle and untrustworthy bunch; however, the pain of that betrayal sought to bury that lies deep within my soul.

It would be great if I could end this entry by saying that because of the love of God and my maturity, I have never encountered this kind of pain of betrayal again, but it is simply not true. There is nothing new under the sun and the devil's goal is always to discourage and divide us. The truth is that I must continually be intentional about keeping my heart open—first to God and then to his people. I am convicted by God's unfailing, unconditional love for me. I love because he first loved me.

The Risk of Trusting
Cynthia Hawthorne Armstrong

Dear Diary, The years from 2009 to 2013 were some of the most hellaciously painful years of my life. Since love, trust, and betrayal are all matters of the heart, it is no surprise that my Judas experience began with heartbreak.

I had been married since 1989 to a considerably gifted, intelligent preacher committed to the Lord's service. We had been friends. We had weathered his being in seminary together. We were raising a beautiful, intelligent, believing daughter. We had survived a demanding staff position at a fast-growing church, two pastorates, being voted out of a church, and planting a church. We had participated in conferences together, conducted marriage seminars together, ministered at churches together, and enjoyed what I thought was a challenging but fulfilling life together. I thought we were coasting along well in life, but somewhere along the journey, something had changed.

I knew something was amiss because we didn't talk anymore. In fact, he barely acknowledged me, except for grand accolades in front of the church. We barely synchronized calendars. We did not discuss our money. We did not go on dates. And sadly, I couldn't "get no satisfaction." My life consisted of taxiing my daughter and attending her events, working a demanding job, and receiving assignments from my husband about what I was supposed to have done by Sunday. I was a typical small-church pastor's wife—the backup, stand-in, fill-in, auxiliary, assistant everything who was notably dressed. But my marriage was jacked. So, one night, I went to the Lord, the Designer of marriage, the One who knows everything, and asked Him what was wrong.

The next day, on Thanksgiving 2009, the Lord uncovered the most urgent issue in my marriage—my husband was committing adultery and had been for years. I was shocked and dismayed! I had never experienced that level of betrayal. I did not want to lose my family. I did not want my 17-year-old daughter to be damaged. I didn't know what to do, but I knew I wanted to save my marriage, so we tried counseling. Even after having the best counselors, there was no true honesty or authenticity. The trust was broken. I had been betrayed by my husband, my intimate partner in life who was supposed to protect me. After two different Christian marriage counselors, I asked the Lord for release and divorced on biblical grounds that were clearly stated in the divorce decree. A marriage with only one committed party is a contradiction in terms. The marriage was 21 ½ years of my life. The divorce was the end of that chapter, but it was not the end of my life. I thought the next chapter might be tough, but at least it would not have the same misery.

Well, I was right. My life became a different kind of miserable. It resembled the movie *A Series of Unfortunate Events*, and I was definitely the main character. I was divorced and heartbroken. The church plant dissolved. The bank foreclosed on my home. I lost my job. My daughter went to college in another region of the country (a truly empty nest). The Lord blessed me with a good-paying job that allowed me to send one of my two monthly checks for college tuition and live on the other. But I had to leave that job to relocate and help my mother care for my sick, unregenerate father. I relocated and did temp work for a year, which depleted my finances. Then I found a lump on my body. Yes, it was stage three of a very aggressive cancer. One friend said she had never met anyone who had dealt with so many significant issues in so little time. She dubbed me Jobina, because like Job, I got bad news on the heels of other bad news. One disaster happened right after the other and I felt betrayed.

The obvious betrayal was from my spouse. He breached the trust and sanctity of our marriage. What had I done wrong? Why didn't I know? The enemy of our souls, the accuser, told me that it was my fault, that I was not enough, and that I could have done something to prevent it.

The enemy used friends, church members, the Christian community, and even family to attack me. I had not expected more betrayal, but I was especially taken aback by the betrayal at the hands, or rather mouths, of church folk. The church, in general, does not handle divorce well, but it really has a hard time with ministry divorces. I encountered those who had no problem blaming or victimizing the victim. I was asked under whose authority did I think I could divorce my husband. I was told that I should be more spiritual and forgiving of his "indiscretion." I was told that I would be sinning if I divorced him and that if I really forgave him, I would stay. I even had gossip mongers, who didn't really talk to me before, call and ask how I was, in hopes that I would share juicy details. (I got so quiet that we could hear crickets.) There were even those who said that it must have been something I did to make him turn to someone else. What!?!

Then everything stopped. My house went from Grand Central Station to a ghost town. My house phone used to ring all the time. It stopped so abruptly that I picked it up to see if the thing was still working! I was suddenly all by myself. I felt isolated, but I was actually insulated. The Lord was protecting me from the onslaught of the enemy. I was even more isolated after my relocation and again during my illness. It was all necessary so that I could be alone with the Lord and be comforted and healed by Him.

It was during my times alone with Jesus that I realized and acknowledged that I felt betrayed by the Lord. It was also during this time that, like Job, I asked the Lord troublesome questions and He gave me forthright answers.

- Lord, why did You let this happen?
  The Holy Spirit guides and warns the believer, but each man has free will and chooses to do right or wrong.
- Lord, what did I do wrong?
  I was not flawless, but I am not to blame for another person's choice
- Why didn't You tell me?
  He revealed it to me when I asked Him and when I could handle the answer.
- Why did You let this continue so long?
  Because the Lord loves all his children, He was extending grace and mercy to my brother to give him time to choose right.
- What now, Lord?
  He let me know that I needed to continue to forgive, heal and grow. He then wanted me to minister, serve, and focus on His purpose for my life.

The Lord Jesus carried me through all the heartache, the mental duress, the ravaging illness, and the humbling lack, and He grew me up! But I had to put on my big girl clothes and face what was facing me with a heart surrendered to the Lord.

First, I got more into God's Word and spent time with Him. Running to the Holy Bible and not from it in times of trouble is crucial to spiritual healing. It was essential that I trust the Lord. He did not betray me, even though it felt like He did. My feelings were frazzled. My faith was foundational. I studied John 13 in which Judas betrayed Jesus. Since

Jesus was fully God and fully man, He knew that Judas would betray Him. I could not imagine knowing from the beginning that I would be betrayed. Yet Jesus gives the example of continuing in and fulfilling His purpose and bringing God glory. God's Word helped me remember that I can trust the Lord completely.

I also made sure I had a spiritual covering, with both a Christian church and a small circle of godly friends. Although I felt betrayed by the church, I was still encouraged to participate in corporate assembly and worship. When the church plant dissolved, I joined a local church. Before I relocated, I researched online and found my current church. In both cases, I had a caring, watchful shepherd who taught me and fed me with God's Word. I had to take the risk of being in the body of Christ. The trials I dealt with from some frenemies and religious people only served to identify a circle of women I could trust. This small circle of godly women surrounded me, listened to me, walked with me through each transition, and prayed for me, especially during my biweekly chemo treatments.

Two of those friends are licensed Christian counselors. In John 11, Jesus raised Lazarus from the dead and told his community to lose him and let him go. He was alive but was still bound by his grave clothes. Christian counseling is valuable. It is a part of removing the grave clothes after we are raised to new life. Christian counselors help us get our thinking straight after trauma or just after dealing with the issues of our childhood. I still talk to a counselor periodically, just like I get a physical annually.

Ultimately, I just had to grow to trust again. We are seldom betrayed by someone that we do not trust. I have heard the saying, "Get me once, your fault. Get me twice, my fault." I agree with learning to be more watchful, but if I allowed what happened to me to change the way I love, trust, or serve, I am giving away more power to those who hurt me. I could continue to ruminate on the trauma, but I had to let it go. A good marriage requires trust. Church fellowship, ministry, and service are enhanced by trusting. Betrayal is the risk of trusting, but it is not always the outcome. Human parents, spouses, children, and friends choose to betray when they choose themselves over you. They did not start out to be that person, but they became that person. You are not at fault for their decision. There is only One who is trustworthy. There is only One who is willing and able to keep every promise. And I trust Him, the Lord Jesus Christ, who never left me.

And now, by God's grace, several years after I was ditched, divorced, dislodged, displaced, and diseased, I stand healed, content, victorious, joyful, with a forgiving spirit, and most of all, a grateful heart! I stand ready and focused on comforting others with the comfort I received so that He may get what He intended all along...to God be the glory!

Judas Among Us
Shirley A. Wilson

Dear Diary, We didn't typically go visiting on a weekday evening, but this was an exception, and I was along for the ride. The house wasn't too far from the church; we parked alongside the road in front of the home of the new associate minister and his family. Pleasantries were exchanged, hospitality extended, and light banter ensued. My dad used to say, "Little pitchers have big ears." He was right because I sat on their soft and comfy couch drinking in every bit of grown folks' conversation.

From what my teenage mind could piece together, there was conflict brewing in our church surrounding the lifestyle choices of one of our key leaders. Some of the membership did not cotton much to pastoral confrontation on the matter but instead viewed it as a personal attack on the sister to whom some were related. From what I gathered, some of the membership planned to challenge the pastor at an upcoming business meeting.

In the silence, during the ride home, the aha moment came. They planned to vote the current pastor out and replace him with a new pastor. The associate pastor would then become the new pastor, and the leader in question would not have to face church discipline. A masterful, well-disguised coup d'état. Our visit was, in actuality, a fact-finding mission—finding out where this minister stood in all this. While he voiced undying support, several books regarding how to be an effective pastor were neatly housed on the nearby bookshelf.

Next Sunday, the sermon was boldly declared, "For I have not shunned to preach the whole Gospel..." After which, a letter of resignation was read. That was our last Sunday as pastor and the first family of that church. Up until that time, I viewed church life through idyllic lenses. I loved spending time in the place with the people who, up until that time, represented extended family to me. One thing I learned from this particular experience is that even people who worship together can and do wound each other. I saw firsthand the pain such wounds could cause. Even though we had to move on and find a new church and a new congregation, I tucked those people and that experience into a corner of my heart for safekeeping and reference when needed under a file labeled JUDAS.

Judas is not always easy to identify. Like Judas of Scripture, she or he slides into the inner circle and is privy to the actions, motivations, and intentions of the infiltrated group or person. Since we do not readily have the same powers of identification that our Savior demonstrated during His earthly ministry, we, unfortunately, don't always find out about Judas before the betrayal occurs. Meanwhile, he has become one of us, with his decisions and deeds directly affecting us somehow.

Three years after my husband completed his seminary education, he worked full-time as a staff pastor at the prestigious Concord Missionary Baptist Church in Dallas, Texas, pastored by the late Rev. Dr. EK Bailey. This church was triple the size of any church we attended in Pennsylvania, and it was our first time experiencing full-time pastoral ministry. We both fell in love with the pastor, his family, and the people. A preacher par excellence, a pastor's pastor, Dr. Bailey, and his beautiful wife, Dr. Sheila Bailey, were solid mentors to us. I like to say that we "grew up" in our marriage and ministry during our tenure at that church. As comfortable as it was under this great pastor, my husband had a vision to start a church in our home state of Pennsylvania within a 20-mile radius of our town. In a unique step of faith, we transitioned back home.

Once we got settled, my hubby began to share his vision with friends who voiced genuine interest in his preaching/teaching ministry. He had invited those we considered dear friends, many of whom pledged allegiance to the vision BEFORE we even left for seminary. We would periodically check in with these individuals, assuring them of our continued commitment and intention to plant a church in the near future. Naturally, we invited them to our vision-casting meetings. Strangely, we did not get the same reception regarding the vision. Some suggested we get further training back at our home church; I guess four years of seminary and seven years as full-time pastoral staff wasn't enough. Others avoided us like the plague, ignoring our calls, reluctant to tell us they were no longer interested in joining the work. From some friends, we even got, "How dare you come into town to start a church without checking with me!" It was hard not to take these responses as a betrayal of sorts. After all, we were the same people they believed in before we left for seminary. We soon learned that God is fully aware of it all. Try as he might, Judas cannot stop the will or work of God. Out of the 60-plus people with whom we met, God chose seven people who were willing to step out on faith with our family. This core group planned and strategized with us for an entire year. On July 7, 1996, Christian Faith Fellowship launched its first worship service. It wasn't until many years later that we once again encountered Judas.

In pastoring, we have discovered that people come and go for various reasons. Sadly, some leave through death. Others leave because of a perceived personal insult they have chosen not to reveal. Instead, they slip away, never to be seen in the congregation again. Still, others are very vocal to the congregation regarding their opinions or issues, but with the pastor, not so much. Those are the most hurtful. No matter how much you have served this person and their family, they would rather be the judge, jury, and executioner of the pastor while collecting supporters of their version of events. What really hurts is when those who have been extremely close, dedicated, and loyal to the work and could easily validate the true heart of the pastor simply will not. Instead, they become diehard supporters of such individuals who cannot and have not articulated their issues with the pastor personally.

It seems that maintaining a friendship with such individuals is more important to them than defending the person who watches over their very souls. A lot of them choose to play both sides. How can they be loyal to the pastor and loyal to a person who discredits the pastor every chance he or she gets even well after that person has left the church? It gives off Judas vibes. Et tu, my brother or sister in Christ?

We faced this situation for a time or two. The most hurtful involved a lifelong mentor, friend, and core group member instrumental in the early growth of our church. Time and space do not permit a full accounting of his contribution to our church over the years. As his health declined, depriving him of his full faculties and participation, the pastor encouraged members to reach out to meet the needs of him and his wife, which they did, providing haircuts and respite breaks for the wife, meals, visits, and such. Who would not welcome such support? After all, being a caregiver 24/7 is draining and difficult.

One day, the church mail contained a scathing letter to the pastor demanding to end her husband's affiliation with the church he helped to plant. She wanted his name removed from the roll and asked that the pastor no longer visit him. No explanation was given. Two whole years later, he died. A few of the members called to tell us; otherwise, we would never have known. The church where he had so faithfully served was not permitted to participate in his home-going. His faithful, 20-year affiliation with our church was ignored in the obituary and general reflections. There was no mention of the pastor with which he so faithfully served. Instead, the widow invited former members to give reflections on this great man and our dear friend. Another pastor preached the eulogy; he barely knew him. As difficult as it was, we went to the viewing to pay our respects, even though we were told that the funeral was private, despite the fact that it was held in a large community church. Our conspicuous absence was fodder for many a conversation. Encounters with Judas have left us deeply wounded. Thankfully, our God heals the penetrating wounds created by such encounters.

Judas Summary
Christine O. James

A Closing Point of View:

I love to love people. Frequently, when I meet new people, I can be like a little puppy, wagging my tail, waiting to see what new adventures we might share together. As I have reflected upon some of the "Judas" of my life, they were all people who I really enjoyed in one way or another. They were often funny, smart and talented. A real joy to be around.

Gifted people with good intentions can be troublesome if their gifts are not yielded to the Spirit of God. Betrayal from the people we love comes at a high cost to our hearts. I've watched as people who started out as humble servants allow ambitious pride to cause them to manifest behaviors that quickly become divisive and destructive. I choose to believe that they don't start off with such evil intent, but when they believe they have a better way, they do everything within their power to fight for their way, even if it is in direct opposition to God's way, as communicated by God's servant.

To avoid betrayal, many pastors' wives don't go deep with very many people. There are times when I meet another pastor's wife and ask her how she is doing and they give the simple cursory answer, "I'm good."

The look they often give me after I ask is, "Who are you? I don't know you. I have nothing further to say." And I get it. I have definitely had my little heart broken on more than one occasion for sharing with people who were not careful with my trust.

But here is a nugget of wisdom that I shared with my daughter after a painful breakup she went through many years ago. I told her, "Never apologize for loving someone. The privilege of loving is a great gift from God. What people do with that gift is not our responsibility; it's between them and God." This is an encouragement that I must frequently give to myself as well. I choose to courageously love rather than be bitter and barren. Jesus told us that the world will recognize us by our love for one another. He modeled this for us as he ate with Judas and washed his dirty feet. He knew what he was going to do, but he served him anyway. Jesus loved and served because he knew that the Father's plan was still in full effect. The same is true for us. God always has a plan for our pain. It's all working together for our good because we love Him and we are called according to purpose.

Scriptures for Prayerful Reflection:

> And we know that in all things God works for the good of those who love him, who have been called according to his purpose. For those God foreknew he also predestined to be conformed to the image of his Son, that he might be the firstborn among many brothers and sisters.
>
> ~ Romans 8:28-29 NIV

> My companion attacks his friends;
> he violates his covenant. His talk is smooth as butter,
> yet war is in his heart;
> his words are more soothing than oil,
> yet they are drawn swords. Cast your cares on the Lord
> and he will sustain you;
> he will never let the righteous be shaken.
>
> ~ Psalm 55:20-22 NIV

> Therefore, as God's chosen people, holy and dearly loved, clothe yourselves with compassion, kindness, humility, gentleness and patience. Bear with each other and forgive one another if any of you has a grievance against someone. Forgive as the Lord forgave you. And over all these virtues put on love, which binds them all together in perfect unity.
>
> ~ Colossians 3:12-14 NIV

Let Us Pray Together:

Lord, I thank you that being a community of believers was your idea. You told us that two are better than one. We need one another's care and concern to help us along the journey of life. We need the fellowship and friendships that model your unfailing love to the world despite our differences. God, when our humanity causes pain, help us to trust you, the healer of broken hearts. Help us not to be self-protective but rather trust you in all things. We know that our thoughts are not your thoughts, nor your ways our ways, so we give ourselves afresh to you. And in those moments we find ourselves sitting at the table of betrayal, we will trust your divine purpose through it all. Amen.

JUDGMENT
Contributors

Introduction
Dr. Larry L. Anderson Jr.

Falling Forward
Tamara Washington

Judgment, No Judgment
Telisha Acklin

I Come Not to Judge
Cynthia W. King

It Comes with the Job
Rebecca Watson Autry

Judgment Summary
Christine O. James

Introduction
Dr. Larry L Anderson Jr.

Out of all the topics I selected for this book, there was one topic the pastors' wives unanimously agreed to have encountered: judgment. Of course, as a pastor I'm aware of the fishbowl that my wife and family were placed in when we became the first family of the church. For some reason the pastor's family is expected to be the holiest, the most spiritual and the closest thing to perfection that the Lord could find. And they are expected to flawlessly embody and display all of the fruits and gifts of the Spirit for the rest of the church to inspect and respect. In *The Pastors' Diaries*, this judgment was dealt with from the pastor's perspective, and in the forthcoming book *The Pastor's Kids' Diaries*, you'll get an opportunity to hear how it affected them, but right now, this is all about the wives. The wives who are examined through the microscope of human eyes and opinions. Their hair length, their skirt length, their shade of lipstick, whether they have their shoulders and arms out or a V-neck shirt is all seen through a lens of conservatism or risqué. The way they speak, how much they speak, how little they speak. Why are they leading, why are they not leading—it's all being judged. There is not a time when they can look around the room and not catch someone looking back at them and forming an opinion because this is the fishbowl of judgment for the first lady.

Armed with the knowledge of the expectations of pastors' wives, I decided from the moment that I said yes to accepting the position of pastor, it came with the condition of allowing my wife to be Kim. Not First Lady Kim, not Music Ministry Leader Kim, not Women's Ministry Leader Kim, not Co-Pastor Kim, just Kim. I requested that they allow her to be a member of the body who can grow and be discipled, who can love the Lord and serve the Lord just like them. I shared that she was a faithful woman who loved me and our children and she needed a church and community just like each of them needed. The church embraced our transparency and the lack of preferential treatment and expectations my family desired, and they treated Kim like any other woman.

The only problem was Kim was not any other woman. Kim was the woman who was sharing her husband with the entire church. Kim's confidant is now the church's confidant. Kim sits at the dinner table with an empty chair across from her because her husband is at a meeting at the church. Kim's honey-do list grows to infinity because Saturdays are dedicated to sermon prep as her co-vocational husband works another full-time job, which prohibits him from working on it during the week. Kim's husband is preaching, teaching, counseling, leading, planning, discipling, while Kim, with a full-time job herself, feels she is being forced to handle almost everything in their home alone, including the raising of their children. Kim, like so many other pastor wives, has a husband who now has two full-time jobs and is on call 24 hours to a church that is not able to sustain them financially and cannot afford to provide their family with health benefits. So maybe Kim shouldn't be treated like any other woman because no other woman is sacrificing nearly as much for the church. It's not a "first lady" title or a front-row seat; it's not a special parking space or a big hat that Kim or any pastor's wife needs—it's respect. These wives need the compassion and consideration of the church to understand boundaries when it comes to their husbands. They need the church not to judge them for missing a church function when the church is the one who is responsible for them being burned out because they have had to do so much without their husbands. They need grace, not dirty looks when they show up late to church with three kids dressed, and yet their husband is praised because he was at church an hour early—he only needed to get himself dressed. They need vacation time, grace, love, and honor so they don't grow bitter and begin to judge the church that has been judging them. They need not be ignored because they cannot lead a ministry or take on even more responsibilities in the church; they need to be invited and welcomed to always get in where they see themselves fitting in by a community that loves them and understands their plight.

The question I wrestled with so much in interviewing women for this book is, "Why?" Why is the pastor's wife so heavily scrutinized? Is it jealousy? Do all the women in the church really feel they should be in their place? Is it the rich history of the church's great "first ladies" and the inability of their current first lady to live up to it? Is it the history of difficult and prideful first ladies and the determination to keep their current one in her place? There were so many ideas and reasons that surfaced but the one thought that kept coming back to my mind came from Genesis 3. The Bible shares that the satanic attack on the first family began with the enemy going after Eve in the Garden of Eden. We must recognize the spiritual warfare that tempts us subconsciously as a church to destroy our leadership and the family structure that the Lord has put in place to guide us. To say you love and pray for your pastor and not love and pray for his wife is not truly loving him at all. We have all heard that an unhappy wife can make an unhappy life, and therefore, the blessing of pastoring can easily become the burden of their existence when the entire family is not loved and embraced by the body. Remember, the pastor's wife is your sister in Christ and the daughter of God the Father. She has been placed where she is by Him and for Him. To do anything to demean, disrupt, or destroy that is to do the work of the enemy, and coincidentally, that normally starts with sinful judgment.

Falling Forward
Tamara Washington

Dear Diary, It has always been easy to play the victim. It's comfortable to look beside me and blame that person for my actions. But what do you do when you've played a role in the failure of a relationship? What do you do when believers are affected by your actions and decide to leave your local church? It's comfortable to blame others, but I know better. I know I ought to be careful with my tongue because, as the Bible says, the tongue can be "an unruly evil, full of deadly poison" (James 3:8b). I knew this, and yet I allowed my flesh to do what it so desired. Here is what happened.

A few years ago, my husband decided to lead a discipleship group for several married men in our church. He asked me to pray about simultaneously leading a discipleship group for their wives. I knew I needed to proceed with this discipleship group, but I was afraid for several reasons. For starters, I was afraid of leading and failing; being the one everyone looked to for guidance and direction has always been a struggle for me. If I'm being honest, I felt that I needed to be discipled, not the other way around. Secondly, I was afraid of getting close to women. While I have always enjoyed social interaction, I have learned over the years not to trust people and to keep them at a distance to protect myself from being hurt.

After becoming a Christian, I even guarded myself in the church. However, I knew if I was going to start this discipleship group, I would have to be 100 percent transparent, especially if I expected the ladies to feel safe in opening up about their personal lives. Finally, I was afraid of the ladies seeing my flaws. I was uncertain of how they would react. There are lofty expectations for pastors' wives. Oftentimes people expect you to be perfect, not realizing that you struggle just as they do and that God is working out imperfections in you as He is in them. Nevertheless, I eventually realized that God wanted to use the discipleship group to draw each of us closer to Him; it was not about me. I needed to just say "Yes," and so I did.

The group consisted of four wives: Maria, who was a new believer; Luisa and Meredith, who had been walking with the Lord for years; and Tonya, a lady who once walked away from the Lord but had recently rededicated her life. We were young and very excited about growing in our walk with the Lord, and we felt Him in our midst from the very beginning. As we spent time in the Word, praying, and sharing our hearts, we felt ourselves getting closer to Him. We challenged each other in our spiritual walk, and we held each other accountable in our marriages. It was a fun time, and we had developed a friendship that became special to me—one that I was excited about. My guard was down, and I cared for each lady. I cherished the times when we shared our hearts together in prayer.

I remember the one time we all got on our knees on my living room floor and began to enter God's presence, recognizing God for who He is and asking Him to move. We were interceding on behalf of our husbands and our children, asking God for wisdom to be a godly influence on our children and God-honoring wives. I also cherished the times our families got together. Whether it was a game of family basketball or going to each couple's house to eat and play board games, or going to an amusement park, we were connecting with God and connecting with one another. It was a beautiful season!

But then it all suddenly changed. Meredith's husband, who was a member of my husband's discipleship group, had financially taken advantage of another member of our church. The incident led to church discipline, and it became so serious that my husband and I sat down with both Meredith and her husband to resolve it, but it did not go well. I can say I went from concerned and hopeful to irritated and vengeful. Things had not gone as planned. There was no brokenness, no repentance, and no desire to resolve the issue. I was upset; I allowed my flesh to take over and I lost my temper.

Dealing with tough issues can be difficult and holding each other accountable in the church can often become messy. Accountability is a word we often don't embrace but desperately need. On the other hand, grace and patience are also crucial and cannot be neglected. God showed me where I went wrong. It was so clear. The Word says, "Convince, rebuke, exhort, with all longsuffering and teaching" (2 Timothy 4:2c NKJV). I forgot to apply the latter part of that verse, and by hurting my sister in Christ, I had offended God. As I thought about what happened, it became clear my sister needed to be heard, and she needed to be met with love and forgiveness from a friend. She needed a kind and gentle response instead of a harsh word that was intended to pierce her heart and shut her down. "A soft answer turns away wrath, but a harsh word stirs up anger" (Proverbs 15:1 NKJV). God could've used me to be an accountable friend, but I lost that privilege. Both Meredith and Maria left the discipleship group and, ultimately, our church. I was devastated. I had no idea my actions would have such severe consequences. I felt like a failure and that God was disappointed in me as a leader. So, with a sincere heart, I asked my heavenly Father to forgive me.

I asked for forgiveness for hurting His daughter and not caring at the time. I asked Him to forgive me for allowing my anger to take over and unload everything I had felt about her. I asked Him to forgive me for allowing my actions to negatively affect a new believer as well. And like a good Father, full of grace and mercy, He did exactly that. The Bible says, "As far as the east is from the west, so far has He removed our transgressions from us" (Psalm 103:12 NASB1955). I also confessed my sin to each lady in the group, including the one directly involved. I shared with them what God had shown me; I was wrong for losing my temper and not controlling my tongue. I asked for their forgiveness, and they forgave me. The Bible says, "Confess your trespasses to one another, and pray for one another, that you may be healed" (James 5:16 NKJV). Even though it was not the same without the entire group, I continued with the remaining ladies, and we continued to grow spiritually.

Even as I reflect on this story now, the very things I feared about starting the group came true. I feared failure, and to some degree, I had failed to lead the group well. I feared being transparent only to be let down later, and I was. I feared my flaws were being exposed, and they were. However, through this experience, I learned how to fall forward by not repeating the same mistake. I also learned valuable lessons that continue with me even to the present. It's okay to challenge yourself, even if you feel unqualified. It's okay to be transparent and show your true self. It's okay for people to see that you are still a work in progress, as we all are. If God gives you the green light, you must proceed. If you fail, recognize it, repent, focus your eyes on Jesus, and keep moving forward. I am so thankful that all things work together for the good of those who love God and who are called according to His purpose (Romans 8:28). Even my missteps. And this is my prayer for both women who left our local church, that God would also redeem this incident in their lives for their good and His glory. Amen.

Judgment, No Judgment
Telisha Acklin

Dear Diary, Navigating life within the church, particularly as a pastor's wife, has been a profound journey filled with both beauty and challenges. What many fail to realize is that when you've grown up alongside the same community your whole life, expectations tend to loom large. This unique situation presents a spiritual challenge, one that urges us to extend the benefit of doubt, for we often believe we know someone so intimately that we have preconceived notions about their actions and character.

The decision to marry my husband sparked various opinions, both positive and critical, adding layers of complexity to our journey. I remember the very moment he walked into the church. There was an inexplicable connection that transcended the ordinary. His attire, the way he carried himself, and the gaze he cast upon me as he walked up to the pulpit from the audience suggested a divine alignment, a realization that he was the man God had chosen for me. However, my initial response was marked by apprehension and a deliberate attempt to avoid the inevitable. I avoided this man like the plague. The idea of marrying a minister, particularly one who would draw attention to my love life within the church, seemed overwhelming. Despite my efforts to sidestep this connection, God's plan and the persistence of the man of God prevailed.

The vivid memory of our first encounter at the pulpit, with exchanged glances and a blush on my cheeks, is etched in my mind. I remember looking away, trying to avoid him, but he pursued me. Our journey transitioned into casual conversations, which evolved into lunch dates and then to dinner dates. The unfolding of our relationship mirrored the subtle yet relentless pursuit of God's plan. Navigating societal expectations and personal reservations, our story became a testament to the transformative power of divine guidance. Embracing the idea of a life with this chosen man led us from avoidance to commitment, challenging preconceived notions along the way. Despite the initial hesitations, our union unfolded in accordance with God's design, demonstrating a love that surpassed earthly judgments anchored firmly in the sacred covenant of marriage.

As a young woman who had essentially been nurtured by the same churchgoers who would now look up to me as their first lady, I became the subject of considerable scrutiny. Was she truly prepared? Some saw me as a child. Others deemed me spoiled. A few even questioned my audacity. And, naturally, the "Why her?" sentiment echoed. What many do not realize is that often, the people making these judgments aren't aware of the weight of their words or the pressure they inadvertently place upon us. Their internal struggles to adapt to the changes around them sometimes manifest as judgment. Yes, it hurt. It left me feeling self-conscious and with a changed perspective. Now, I found myself on the other side of the coin. I never truly understood how it felt to be a first lady or a part of the pastor's family until I was in those shoes. My dad has been a deacon my whole life, but it's totally different. The constant considerations and heightened awareness stem from the fact that people hold you, your husband, your children, and your relationship with God to a unique and elevated standard. Over time, I came to realize that few truly comprehend the challenges faced by a pastor's family despite their well-intentioned empathy. Even our closest relatives try their best to shield us; however, they don't fully understand the weight of the position.

Through the journey of enduring judgment and personal growth, I've come to understand that this process shapes us. The truth is, that people, for the most part, have good intentions. Even when their words sound harsh, first ladies often feel the need to shield their children, husbands, or themselves. Frequently, we perceive these situations as people being recklessly critical. However, as the Scriptures remind us, everything works together for our good.

Congregation members and individuals outside the clergy may not fully grasp the impact their words can have on your children. Often, they overlook the fact that the pastor shoulders blame when situations beyond their control arise, leading to mental strain and self-doubt. When the First Lady, despite her efforts, cannot alter these circumstances and can only turn to God for His protective covering over her family, it brings about considerable stress. I say this because, through these experiences, we learn how to love others, how to help them grow, how to set healthy boundaries, and, most importantly, we come to realize that only God's opinion truly matters. The judgment we face from those imagining how they would act in our shoes is, in fact, a work of fiction in their minds. Living in that reality, in real-time, unveils the truth. Our goal is to follow God's calling, acknowledging that judgment is an integral part of the journey.

I'm the kind of person who chooses to see the best in others, and if their intent is not pure, I trust that God will intervene. It's not my place to concern myself with others' opinions of my family. That's God's domain. Focusing on this perspective, I've learned that those tearful nights, those moments when I felt compelled to engage in verbal battles, and those instances of loneliness that arose from trying to conform to others' expectations when I was just 25, were all part of my journey. They were guiding me to a place where I could sow the seeds of empathy, patience, love, and kindness openly so that those observing us could witness how God desires us to care for one another.

As we navigate the path set by God, it's crucial to recognize His constant presence with us. He assures us that He is shaping and molding us. A saying I particularly cherish is, "It only takes one moment in time for our lives to change." Therefore, our aim is to live with the conviction that we serve a God who never forsakes us; He has ordained us for the role of first ladies. God is fully aware of the challenges and judgments that come our way. He understands that we possess the strength to lean into His love and guidance during the days of scrutiny. Living with the assurance that He has placed us in this position for a purpose, actively molding and shaping us, allows us to emerge from every experience stronger and greater.

This year marks our 20th wedding anniversary, a journey that began with our engagement just six weeks into dating and our marriage within nine months. Life, however, hasn't always been smooth. Serving the church has brought both judgment and high praise, yet our love for the people and dedication to the Lord's work remains unwavering. Our journey teaches the same members we serve how to live with the judgment of others, but most of all, how to judge less. This path isn't always easy; it entails stumbling and rising again. Yet, it undeniably generates more love and less judgment within our congregation.

I Come Not to Judge
Cynthia W. King

Dear Diary, The question I pose to myself today is, "What would I say to my younger self who is in the throes of becoming the wife of a pastor?" I would say, "Enjoy the journey and expect the unexpected." Of course, centering on those words of wisdom would be based on the foundation of my maturity and willingness to see from a perspective that is higher than mine.

Often, we are judged by our outward appearance. In ministry, as the wife of a pastor, we are judged by the clothing we wear, our hairstyles, the type of home we live in or the car we drive, whether we "craft" or bake the homemade jams and jellies, work in or out of the home, are hospitable, and how we love on our husbands and children. Oh, and let's not forget the ultimate prerequisite for the traditional church: singing and playing the piano.

This entry is infused with celebration and reflections on the journey, the maturity, and seasons of ever-changing perspectives. It is hard to imagine that we are in the process of celebrating 30 years of my husband being the pastor of the same church. Reviewing the snapshots of the highs and lows, the good and bad, the trials and triumphs has been fulfilling. It has been a journey of perpetual evolution. I have taken ownership of the fact that I have changed and embraced it as a good thing. It has been awesome to be able to be a beacon of light in darkness. Admittedly, embracing the evolving of self in this role was not due to one specific situation, position or circumstance but my maturity in my relationship with my Savior.

Totally working through who and whose I am and what HIS purpose was for me has been empowering. To further drive it home, I would encourage myself in this role to keep first things first. By that, the number one priority/mission would be securing a strong and more intimate relationship with God. I am a product of growing up and being nurtured right in the middle of the twentieth century, a baby boomer, and still growing. As one who has a rich history in church, religion, traditions, Jim Crow, peace, love, and power to the people, I have seen the evolution of changing cultures within the role of the pastor's wife. Surprisingly, though, there is still nothing new under the sun. And, as penned by Andraé Crouch, "Through it all, I 've learned to trust in Jesus, I've learned to trust in God."

New marriage, new mother, new ministry wife all within the first year of marriage, along with new judges and jurists. Seven weeks into our marriage and two weeks before my husband was to be licensed, we discovered we were five weeks pregnant. Several members of the church we were attending had the audacity and the boldness to ask me if I was pregnant before I got married. My response in today's culture would be, "Where do we do this?" or pulling from my familiar phrasing, "Do you know me like that?" Folks were calculating dates and questioning the veracity of our announcement. Lord, is this a prelude for what is to come? Are people going to feel as though they have liberties to say whatever they want and however they want to me? Thank God for parental wise counsel. Although I was unable to articulate it or express it to my "new" husband at the time, I wanted him to pick up the cues telepathically and bravely pronounce, "I, your knight in shining armor, is here to save the day." Well, he was still navigating through the newness of it all too. From the onset, it was obvious that balance in our lives would have to be intentional. Quite honestly, we struggled and were challenged in this area for quite some time. The level of intentionality regarding balance in our lives was especially important to me.

At the age of nineteen, my parents separated and thus ended their marriage, and somewhere in the recesses of my mind, I attributed it to being so busy in life. The impact of that event had been tucked away and resurfaced after I was now married. As the wife of a pastor, after God and loving Jesus, my primary role was to love and be a submissive wife to my husband, a mother, a grandmother and sister in Christ, etc. These roles gave me so much experience in building more godly character and exercising the fruit of the Spirit. I had always secretly entertained the desire not to live a very public life due to growing up with parents who were actively involved not only in the service of the Kingdom but were entrepreneurs as well and had several businesses that often required a lot of time and attention. Please do not misinterpret, as there was strong familial support. However, I desired not to live a life that was in full display of onlookers. Well, Jeremiah 29:11 NIV states, "'For I know the plans I have for you,' declares the Lord, 'plans to prosper you and not to harm you, plans to give you hope and a future.'" Ironically, everything that had occurred in my life leading up to becoming Mrs. King was a part of the plan—from tasks and assignments given to carry out in the stores they operated to the leadership development curriculums we participated in within our denomination on a local and national level.

One of the most rewarding environments for me as a pastor's wife was the sweet fellowship and relationships I established with other pastor wives over the past 41 years. Often, many refer to life in the ministry as living in a fishbowl. The round circumference of an open sphere that is on display. Those outside the bowl are looking in, and those within the bowl wrestle with the idea that they cannot do anything without people watching and judging you.

As time progressed in this role, I became more intentional in pursuing relationships with those I felt I could relate and identify with, who understood and shared some of the things I may not have necessarily felt comfortable in sharing in the women's ministry. Sometimes sharing or being transparent with some within the congregation had proven to be hurtful and disappointing, and at other times priceless. You are forced into the harsh reality that some are intent on being busybodies and divisive or planting seeds of discord amongst the brethren, and there are those who give authentic and genuine care and concern.

Depending on where you are in your relationship with the Lord, your husband, and anything and anyone else, you can land the plane in operating out of emotions or logic. Let me just say, in the beginning of our journey, it was a very emotional season. And I eventually came to a point of accepting that it was okay. The seeds were germinating for harvest time, and I have now learned to embrace and foster good and healthy relationships in and outside of my church community. No, it is not always cute and wrapped in a perfect bow when you are going through it, for sure. It stings, you doubt, your physical body is impacted, you question your identity, and even entertain thoughts that are not pleasing.

I am truly thankful and grateful for the pastor's wife, whose husband preceded my husband, Mrs. Viola McCoy. Many would often question me about how it was in my role with the previous pastor's wife still attending the church. From my pen to your eyes, a sheer blessing. When I was charged by the late beloved, First Lady Viola McCoy, she told me to be myself and keep the home fire burning. That there were pearls of wisdom. It is my hope that if I'm ever on that same journey, I will imitate that behavior. Sheer grace, elegance, and a love for Christ and his creation. Her charge gave me freedom in the fishbowl to continue evolving and working in the space I am in as I continue to grow and develop in my walk. With that said, I have learned to pivot and do deeper dives, all while being true to who God has called me to be.

Many times, when I thought I did not have the bandwidth to press, I was reminded that I had to press and look upward. Praying a little while longer, seeking His face, and bathing in the book of Proverbs helped me better understand humanity. God has made us uniquely different, and the role of a pastor's wife is not going to fit exactly as that of another ministry wife. However, if you remain true to who you were called to be, room is made for you in the Kingdom to be your authentic "Be You Ti Ful'(beautiful) you in spite of. He knows the plans.

It Comes with the Job
Rebecca Watson Autry

Dear Diary, I clearly remember the first time I heard judgment in someone's tone. I was around five years old and a very close loved one peered down at me and said, "If you keep eating like that, you are going to end up as fat as my niece." I can still hear their tone of voice. I can still feel their disdain for me. The judgment was palpable, and it nips at me to this day. After that, I quickly learned that people judging you is a part of life in this fallen world. As I grew, I learned that women get judged when thriving and even when just surviving. Because of these experiences along the way, I should have been prepared for the judgment that comes with being a pastor's wife, but I was not. The level of entitled judgment thrown at those married to ministers can make you want to run and hide before and after service. It can be as simple as judgment over the pastor's attire because surely you could have ironed better. It can seem as harmless as, "We missed you at the meeting. You must have had something better to do than be with your own church members." It can even be job-threatening and character-crushing, but no matter the kind of judgment, churches seem to have their own particular style of judgment waiting for the pastor and his family.

Early on in our marriage and ministry together, my husband and I dealt with infertility. Twenty years ago, it was talked about even less than it is now, but every year, especially on holidays, I would hear from churchgoers. Their judgments would start as a concern. "How are you holding up watching all these little ones sing in the Christmas choir?" one would voice. I would feel just for a moment seen. Most times, though, it was followed by a right hook. "If you weren't like this or that, you probably would conceive," and "Do you know we built this parsonage to hold up to five children? What a shame it sits empty with just you two." "We probably could get more young families to join if you could just hurry up and start a family," was my personal favorite, as if the population of the church singlehandedly relied on our procreation. On days like Mother's Day and Father's Day, we felt more like a disappointment to the church since we had not provided little feet to run through the church. This seven-year judgment of disappointment did not ruin our love for those we served, but it stung severely.

As God would write our story, the next chapter included building our family through adoption. We spent two years praying and searching for an agency that loved birth mothers and supported them through the hard choices they were making. We prayed and wept, knowing that adoption was not easy on anyone involved, but we knew that God would have us love a child who needed it. As time passed, we shared with our church. With great hope and expectation, we hoped they would be thrilled with our journey to give them a PK (preacher's kid). We shared that we were expecting. Those close to us were so helpful and excited even though we didn't have a normal nine months to prepare, but only ten days. We were shocked and appalled at the other reactions. "Did you speak with the leadership about adopting? Are you going to beg us for money? What if you get a kid who is awful?" Those were real questions I got asked that day.

The hardest and most dreadful judgment came a few days later when people met our child. My son came home, and we instantly became a transracial family because our son was of a different ethnicity. We had sought the Lord, studied, and taken classes on what this would mean for us. We were fully aware of the hardships and the education and hard work it would take for him to feel both loved in our family and accepted in our culture. We were prepared to raise him with the knowledge of both cultures, as our hands were open to the Lord, trusting He would fill in our inadequacies. I say all that to say we were prepared for the world to judge us, but not the church. "No one asked us if you could bring in a Black child to the church," was said to my face. *No one asked, and NO ONE ASKED.* I still sit with those words in my head ringing around when I am in a weak moment. I still grieve it too.

Judgment around our family didn't stop with the choice of adoption. At the time I was serving on staff as part-time choir director and director of music, while my husband served as pastor. When we announced our son was coming home, I asked leadership if I could take maternity leave to get used to motherhood and come back a month later to continue my duties. I was firmly told no. "You did not carry this child in your body, so we do not think you need leave to adjust," was loud and clear. Our son came home on Wednesday, so that Sunday, I sat on the platform empty-handed where an infant should have been. I had left him at home with my lovely and trusted sister-in-law, but it was not the same. We had been instructed that in order to build trust in us as parents, we should be the only ones feeding and changing, and most of the physical touch should come from us for the first month. Yet, there I sat on a platform expected to lovingly bring people to the throne of God and uplift the message prepared by my husband. I sat and cried. I sang and cried. I felt so torn.

After worshiping that very day, I resigned, feeling as though I had no choice. Judgment of others stole from me and the church. Music ministry is my gift and passion, and I did not think it would end that way, but it did. I will never regret going home that day and knowing I would have that early time to adjust as a family with an infant, but I still remember the pain of sitting there with everyone watching.

I wish I could close the story of that church with a beautiful picture of redemption. I can't. The day my husband resigned, there was a group of people who danced out of the church. One used a racial slur in their excitement as we were exiting. That chapter was closed abruptly and in a way, I would have never expected.

After a beautiful season as missionaries planting a church in a city we loved dearly, the church had to close. It was not thriving, and our members needed more. We visited other churches within an hour away, and before long we had shepherded our members to a new flock. It was a bittersweet time of watching the Lord's timing and loving the people more than the moment.

We prayed and hoped to stay in the city, and as it happened, a church of older parishioners asked my husband to come fill in and maybe fill their need for a pastor. We were thrilled and prayed for guidance. At our church plant, I played the piano and led worship. Most Sundays our preschooler would come sit next to me on the piano bench and sing as I led the congregation. It was a sweet time of little distraction in an environment of many young families.

When we visited this new congregation, they were thrilled that they may get a two-for-one deal on a pastor. Being a musician, I was always prepared to serve in this way when needed. The first Sunday I played for this congregation. My preschooler, who was seated alone in the big sanctuary, walked right down the aisle and sat next to me on the piano bench as the congregation sang. This was what he knew to do in worship—draw near to God and Mom all at once. He threw no fit, he did no cartwheels, yet it drew a judgment I had not expected. After the service, a lady came to me and thanked me for playing and then said these words, "Don't worry, when your son learns what a real church is like, he won't bother you anymore during worship. We will teach him how to act." *What a real church is.* That punch to the gut was swift and painful. Not only was she judging my parenting, but she was also judging the last four years of our heart-invested ministry. She was attacking the only way I knew how to parent and serve at the same time. I am not sure what she intended to teach our son, but I am grateful we did not hang around to find out.

With a passionate husband who loves the Lord and has little room for hypocrisy and a teenage son now learning his own way in the faith, judgments will come. But our family will continue to love the Lord and serve Him in his sanctuary. I just wish it was a safer place.

Judgment Summary
Christine O. James

A Closing Point of View:

What is it about us humans that makes us feel the need to judge and evaluate others? We use ourselves as the template or standard for what we believe to be right or wrong. The need to be right is something that I believe is born of insecurity and a fear of the unknown. We use history and former ways of doing things to presume upon God. We want things to stay the same. We want people to behave the same way that we always expected people to behave. If I can see it, I can control it, then there is no need for faith.

Years ago when I began dating my husband, he took me to an event where I would meet many of his friends for the first time. He had been recently licensed to be a minister of the Gospel, and they felt the need to evaluate me alongside him. I don't remember how word got back to me, but there were comments like, "She doesn't look like a minister's wife," whatever that means. I guess they had a picture of what the person connected to my husband should look like, and it was not me. They didn't know me. They didn't know what gifts or talents I possessed. They didn't know my ministry experience or what schools I had attended. But most importantly, they didn't know how much I loved God and was willing to do anything for Him. Including marrying a minister, which I swore I would never do.

People have been evaluating this way from the beginning of time. When God sent Samuel to look for the next king at the house of Jesse, David's father overlooked him as one who could potentially be king. But God doesn't look at the outward appearance; he looks at the heart. The Bible doesn't say how David felt about not being considered by his father, but from a human perspective, being overlooked by the people closest to you can be very discouraging. Judgments can leave lasting wounds in the flesh. Things that people say about us can resonate in our hearts and minds for years.

The antidote to unhealthy, destructive judgment is the presence of God. When we worship and experience God's holiness, it gives us a more accurate assessment of ourselves and others. Much like the prophet Isaiah, when we see God for who he really is, we cry out, "Woe is me, for I am undone..." (Isaiah 6:5 NKJV). God's holy presence reminds me that there is no good thing in me, no starting place for judgment. When I reckon with the fact that I am a recipient of God's amazing grace and mercy, it facilitates grace out of me toward others. The next time we are tempted to judge one another, let's breathe together... Grace in... Grace out.

Scriptures for Prayerful Reflection:

> Speak and act as those who are going to be judged by the law that gives freedom, because judgment without mercy will be shown to anyone who has not been merciful. Mercy triumphs over judgment.
>
> ~ James 2:12-13 NIV

Oh, the depth of the riches of the wisdom and knowledge of God!

How unsearchable his judgments,

and his paths beyond tracing out!

"Who has known the mind of the Lord?

Or who has been his counselor?"

"Who has ever given to God,

that God should repay them?"

For from him and through him and for him are all things.

To him be the glory forever! Amen.

~ Romans 11:33-36 NIV

"For my thoughts are not your thoughts,

neither are your ways my ways,"

declares the Lord.

"As the heavens are higher than the earth,

so are my ways higher than your ways

and my thoughts than your thoughts.

~ Isaiah 55:8-9 NIV

Let's Pray Together:

Oh God, we thank you that there is none like you in all the earth. You are the Most High God, holy and righteous in all of your ways, yet you love us. Thank you that you love us and see us and have prepared a way for us through your son Jesus. You have made provision for all of our weaknesses and that which is unknown to us. How grateful we are that you don't evaluate us as humans do, but when you look at us, you see your son who sacrificed his life for all of our sins and brokenness. We are living in the light of your love. May we shine that same light on others as we move throughout your world. In Jesus' name, Amen.

JEZEBEL
Contributors

Introduction
Dr. Larry L. Anderson Jr.

Encountering Jezebel
Christine O. James

A Spirit of Jezebel
Vallie T. Kirk

Suburban, Not Stupid
Kimberly A. Anderson

Jezebel Summary
Christine O. James

Introduction
Dr. Larry L Anderson Jr.

As a husband and pastor, I recognize that I and my pastoral colleagues must be aware of the Jezebels in our church. Jezebel is bent on evil, and like Satan himself, is there to kill our ministry, steal our joy, and destroy our witness. Therefore, we better not take these Jezebel types lightly. When one hears the name Jezebel, he or she instantly knows it refers to an ungodly woman who can be married or single, rich or poor, educated or ignorant. The Bible has made this name infamous for all eternity. However, as popular as the name Jezebel is, the name is only discussed a few times in the Bible, in First and Second Kings, and then in the Book of Revelation. Many have debated if it is the same woman being discussed in these two accounts or if it is two different women. Some believe it is one woman named Jezebel and another woman who was so ungodly that the Lord referred to her as a Jezebel in the Book of Revelation. Whatever the case, our Lord in the Book of Revelation informs us that Jezebel is an evil seducer who practices sexual immorality, and this is the first type of Jezebel I want to discuss.

Jezebel was like a daughter to me. I've known her since she was a young girl, maybe just twelve or thirteen years old. I saw such promise and hope on her face, and I saw her desire to be happy. She came into the church full of energy and ideas. She was willing to participate in any and all activities the church would have. Some young people would be shy or hesitant to get involved, but not Jezebel. She would not only get involved, but she would make suggestions on how our church events could cater more to young people. Over the course of time, some very unfortunate circumstances interrupted the family life and structure of Jezebel's home. The church prayed for them, supported them, and let her know she still had a spiritual family and home here at the church. Jezebel seemed to survive the trauma that divided her family as time moved on.

Jezebel returned to the church following her college years, but something was noticeably different. The pure and innocent young girl we remembered had morphed into a young woman who was seemingly battling with her worldly desires and her challenging upbringing. As a father figure and her pastor, I tried to shepherd and discover what her challenges were. She shared a lot of painful memories she encountered during her formative years and her anger, hurt, and disappointments. I felt the magnitude of pain she expressed warranted professional help and an older woman's attention. Therefore, I suggested therapy and assigned her a deaconess to confide in. I believed these things were happening and helping until a few incidents happened at church. There were incidents being reported that, in my opinion, were totally out of character for this young lady. I did not want to believe them or accept them. However, our pastoral team and deaconesses investigated the matters and found the sources credible and the actions sinful. Church discipline is about restoration, not condemnation, so as any good pastor would do, we pursued reconciliation with the parties involved and proper discipline and restoration of Jezebel.

As time passed, the leadership team became aware of a series of unfortunate, sinful events involving Jezebel and others. With each event, the church leadership would go through the same investigation, attempt at reconciliation, discipline, and restoration. The challenging question that began to surface was how many times can we allow these types of incidents to occur? The reality is if Jezebel were a man, Jezebel would have been asked to leave the church. But she was like a daughter to me and others, and we desperately wanted her to win this spiritual battle she was entangled in. However, we also knew we had a responsibility to protect the rest of the flock, and we wrestled with discerning if this was really a Matthew 18 scenario where we biblically needed to treat her as a tax collector or an unbeliever. Well, fortunately for us, this was a decision taken out of our hands because following Jezebel's final indiscretion, she decided to leave the church.

In my two decades of pastoring, I never felt as betrayed as I did the day I heard a rumor of Jezebel saying she and I had a sexual relationship and my wife was aware and complicit with the behavior. Now, to be clear, this accusation had been recanted immediately, but the fact that it was even uttered hurt me deeply. I have never been alone with Jezebel or any woman other than my wife, for that matter, to avoid the mere appearance of evil. So, there was no way that could have happened, but I did not need to convince anyone of my behavior. Those who heard this shared it was something she had accused others of for attention several times prior and said I should not take it personally because it's what she does. However, when you have a pastoral call on your life, these accusations are taken seriously. How could someone I invested so much in be so careless and make such an egregious statement that could have brought every aspect of my life, my character, and my calling into question? To have no idea or concern about what an accusation like that could do to my wife and my children breaks my heart.

My wife, who has always loved young Jezebel and also saw her as a spiritual daughter, felt like she had been stabbed in the back. Her willingness to trust and allow any woman, young or old, to get close to her husband again will be a challenge. She recognized the call and the ministry of a shepherd, but she was furious with the wolf dressed in sheep's clothing. She wondered how much grace we can show to someone who disrespects the pastor and his family in such a way. She wrestles with ever letting anyone get close to us and our family again, and I graciously cannot blame her.

The Jezebel discussed in First and Second Kings is an evil, vicious idolater bent on having her way and destroying the man of God and the Word of God. This second Jezebel at my church was a person who smiled in my face week after week and complimented the Word being preached until the sin they were entangled in, was preached about. However, I had no clue Jezebel was involved in this sin, but the Holy Spirit surely did. I had no clue I had ever offended Jezebel until they left the church and sent me an evil letter accusing me of attacking them from the pulpit. They accused me of being evil and revengeful and ungodly and using the Bible as a weapon of destruction. I was so blindsided by this attack, and I initially wondered if it was a horrible joke. Jezebel's entire row would be the loudest cheering section during my sermons, and just like magic, the entire row disappeared. Jezebel was behind the scenes, poisoning the entire crew with this narrative they had created. The sad part was that none of them ever attempted to have a conversation to check the validity of this false narrative that was being shared; they all just left the church without a goodbye.

It is amazing how much easier it is for some to hear gossip and accept a juicy lie than it is for them to seek the truth. I reached out to a friend that Jezebel and I had in common who had also previously struggled with the sin Jezebel accused me of attacking them about from the pulpit. I knew this mutual friend would communicate that not only did I have a sensitivity for their struggle, but they would be able to clarify that I had no clue that they were struggling with this sinful lifestyle. The next time I saw Jezebel was years later, and they greeted me warmly and humbly. They wanted to pray with me and for me, and I could tell they were apologetic as I could see their embarrassed posture and the overwhelming attention and support they tried to shower upon me. I did not make it difficult for them; just like the father of the prodigal son, all you can do is attempt to forgive and welcome them home. Unfortunately, that would be the last time I saw Jezebel as they passed away shortly after that day.

The truth is I've been attacked over the past twenty years by a few Jezebels, and I have intentionally kept these attacks private and from my wife so that she does not feel a need to defend me in her flesh. But to be honest, to see her naively hug and smile and greet these individuals has caused me some real heartburn. However, in the end, I felt it was better to cover her and keep her heart pure and her mind fixed on the Lord than to allow her to be distracted or fixated on the immaturity and sinful, hypocritical behavior of a few lambs who supposedly love us.

Encountering Jezebel
Christine O. James

Dear Diary, Many years ago, when I was still a young wife and mother, I made the choice to never be distracted by jealousy again. My husband, in my biased opinion, is tall, dark, and handsome, with a deep booming voice used both in preaching and singing. These characteristics are often magnets to women of all ages and sizes. I've watched in awe on various occasions as women would ignore my presence when we were together and approach my husband in a flirty voice, saying, "Pastor, when you sang that song, I felt it in my toes!" or "Pastor, your sermon was so good, you can preach to me anytime!" My silent yet internal response was, "Alright, Miss Thing, I see you!"

My response was not so much about the woman and her behavior but rather the spirit behind the behavior. After years of prayer and study, I've come to realize that those types of interactions are rarely about sexual attraction as Jezebel is often portrayed. Rather the spirit of Jezebel will use whatever tool at her disposal to manipulate and control, including tears, sex, chronic problems, and presenting as a damsel in distress, to realize her end goal. These women may or may not have been attracted to my husband physically, but the real attraction was about his power and authority.

It's important to note that these women are not vixens and villains, although it is very tempting to marginalize them in that way. The behaviors and schemes used by them to get attention can be very problematic and annoying at times, and at other times downright vexing. But the truth is, they are often just broken women with a genuine need for shepherding. However, trauma, mental illness, fear, and shame have taught them coping mechanisms for survival and getting what they want. These coping tools are born of the flesh and easily exploited by the enemy, Satan. The Bible tells us in Ephesians 6:12 NKJV,

"For we do not wrestle against flesh and blood, but ... against the rulers of the darkness of this age, against spiritual hosts of wickedness in the heavenly places."

I've often told my husband that I can tell when a woman has a sincere desire to grow in Christ when they come to our church, not by how they interact with him but by how they relate to me. They can walk around telling people how much they love their pastor and show up faithfully to Bible class and other events that the pastor initiates, but if they avoid me, then, I say, as the Apollo 13 space mission team reported, "Houston, we have a problem!" I know, I know, I can hear people saying, "Well, sometimes women just get along better with men." Stop it! First of all, we are the body of Christ, and secondly, me and my husband are one. If you have a connection with him, you have a connection with me, one way or the other.

One of my first encounters as a married woman encountering Jezebel was in our first pastorate. A woman who was an officer of the church prior to our tenure set her sights on her pastor, my husband, and seemed determined to replace me in his life. She was an attractive yet plain stoic woman, very efficient and helpful in her leadership role. Her demeanor with the pastor was demure, sometimes coy and often giggly as she laughed at the right times in response to his wit and sense of humor.

When we began our service at the church, I had two small boys, one preschool age and an early toddler with another baby on the way. I was due to deliver our baby girl soon after our arrival at the church, so needless to say, I was exhausted. It's important that you have the background story of how I was feeling because it informs how I initially interacted with the situation at hand. Although I was aware of the subtle flirtations of this woman, I honestly didn't have the capacity to do much about it. Then one day I looked up and saw that the woman had totally changed her demeanor. She started dressing like me, wearing the kind of hats and dresses I wore, imitating my best "first lady fashion."

Her interactions with me were standoffish at best and often downright dismissive. She didn't have time for me, and frankly, I didn't have time for her and her intrigues. By this time, I was at the end of my pregnancy with my daughter and could barely walk. Most days, I was just trying to figure out how to put one foot in front of the other—literally. This was my third pregnancy and my belly was huge. It was a very humbling time trying to be poised and present in this new role as the pastor's wife. My sense of self felt like it was being sucked away by the daily demands of two active boys and the little girl on the way. My husband's busy schedule as the new pastor often left me feeling alone in this parenting partnership. He was out doing ministry and I was the keeper of the home. Most days, it felt more like chaos than keeping. Discouragement loomed large, and I felt like an utter failure in all of these new roles.

This blend of circumstances set the stage for the enemy to test my boundaries. I say he was testing my boundaries because he thought I was asleep and unaware. The enemy in the spirit and in the natural thought that I had not noticed how this lady was always trying to position herself to be in my husband's presence. He thought that I didn't notice all of her not-so-subtle flirtations. But I saw it all. I just had to pull up a different set of weapons to fight this battle. I didn't have many carnal (fleshly) weapons at my disposal. I couldn't be cute enough or compete with her in my attire. By this time, I was throwing on anything that fit. Thank God, carnal weapons don't get it done anyway. I needed the mighty through God weapons that pull down strongholds. So, I called down heaven in my prayer life.

Spiritual warfare is ongoing in the lives of the pastor's family. The enemy is always trying to get us to doubt the fact that God is almighty and that He loves us with an everlasting love. So, the enemy often comes for the people we love. He comes to divide our marriages and attack our children, all to distract us from God's calling and purpose. One of the most challenging parts of this purpose is that we have to love even our enemies, those who seek to do us harm. That time presented such an important lesson to me in how to love people but deal fiercely with the devil. One thing I knew then and still know now is that Jezebel could not and cannot be tolerated in our midst. The story of this battle with Jezebel was just the beginning of an intense war that would later ensue within that community. It was the beginning of my recognition that there is always an ongoing battle between darkness and light.

Something that I never thought I would say is how important that time was in my life. Those early entanglements set the stage for who I was to become. I started out in that community as a wide-eyed, naive woman. I believed that if people said they were Christians and loved God, they would love the teaching of His Word and His man and woman servants who delivered the Word. I had no grid for how manipulation and lies could so very quickly come against the purpose of God and His people. What I've come to know is that the enemy always overplays his hand. As the warfare got more intense, so did my prayer life. As people banded together to come against the work of God, it caused me to look to God more in my worship. As I worship, I see God. As I see God, He gives me a purpose-filled perspective about His people. Glory to His name! One thing that I know for sure, no matter what weapon is formed, it will not prosper.

Jezebel has not stopped showing up in our midst. This spirit has shown up on numerous occasions in many different forms and with a variety of agendas. I'm grateful to God that I don't feel quite as visceral about how to engage in these situations. Christ, my firm foundation, continually teaches me how to stand firm and steadfast in the fight. The strategy is simple, yet profound: operate in the opposite spirit. His love never fails.

A Spirit of Jezebel
Vallie T. Kirk

"For our struggle is not against flesh and blood [contending only with physical opponents], but against the rulers, against the powers, against the world forces of this [present] darkness, against the spiritual forces of wickedness in the heavenly (supernatural) places."

Ephesians 6:12 AMP

Dear Diary, Right amid this profound Scripture lures the spirit of Jezebel. Her name is not mentioned here, but she is present. A Jezebel found her way into our dwelling place. The place we call home and the place we love to worship. Jezebel invaded his heart and that crushed mine. It hurt, and it was painful to see his spiritual blindness in this spiritual warfare. This Jezebel showed up during my season of perimenopause, empty nesters, and the death of my father. I truly believed that this season of my life brought her easy access to him, but I know it was not why she showed up.

Jezebel showed up because we were called to minister the gospel of Christ. God was at work in the lives of His servants. God was blessing the lives of His people and souls were saved. Marriages were being restored and the saints of God were changed by the preaching of the gospel of Jesus Christ. Families were joining church together. Worship was astonishing, and as some put it, "It was off the chain!" God was using his servants to grow the church. God was at work, and we positioned ourselves to work alongside our God.

While ministry is flourishing, this Jezebel twitched her way to the pulpit and joined our church. Jezebel came in with her two-piece outfit, an aggressive attraction and a controlling spirit. I needed to pray because he was drawn to the attraction and the control. She piqued his interest. I asked the Lord what I should do with all of this. Do not leave, was His answer. I received that as don't walk away but be still and know that I am God. I heard God speak to my inner self, "I will cover you." I stretched out on the floor in my living room and began to search the Scriptures on God covering us. I read Psalm 91:4, Isaiah 51:16, Deuteronomy 31:8, Psalm 121:3, and many more.

I needed those Scriptures to help me feel secure. It wasn't easy to watch her work her way into his world. She came with some family drama in her life. She set up counseling sessions with her pastor. There were times she would show up at our family outings. I was always surprised to see her there. It was obvious to me she had his attention. I was afraid of losing him to her aggressive attractiveness. I cried a lot. Tearfully, I confronted him with what I saw and what I believed was happening. He assured me nothing was happening, but it was, and I had proof. I also addressed her with proof of her attraction to him. She revealed no denial in her demeanor. I told her to back off in a low yet stern voice while we stood outside in front of the church. She did not back off right away. Jezebel came with an invitation, and I was not on that invite. She continued to show up at church and non-church-related events. Jezebel knew our plans. She was not calling me to see where we were dining or what play we were going to see. She had captured his heart, and he responded to her invitation.

This Jezebel spirit had disrupted my worship at church, and it clouded his judgment on the calling God had given him. I could no longer bear this pain interfering in our personal and spiritual life. What I saw was the old Vallie from my non-Christ days. That Vallie had out-of-control anger issues and a foul mouth. I was angry and afraid. I was afraid for a few reasons. My husband was spiritually blind and needed God to open his eyes to this spiritual attack on our life and our marriage. I was converting back to the old Vallie, and that was very concerning. That lion was trying to devour my husband, God's preacher, and Vallie, His prayer warrior.

I did what I only knew to do; I fasted and prayed. When you let God in the hard places of your life, you are surrendering all to Him. I needed my personal time with Jesus back on track. I wanted NOTHING to separate me from my personal relationship with God. He heard my heart and sent me His Word. Ephesians 4:27 AMP says, "And do not give the devil an opportunity [to lead you into sin by holding a grudge, or nurturing anger, or harboring resentment, or cultivating bitterness]." Listen, I was going to sleep with anger dripping down my mouth. The sun was going down with my wrath, and my nights sometimes became sleepless. I realized my sin was blocking my praise and worship. I forgave them both and continued to trust God to cover us. I continued to pray. It was hard to replace my anger with prayers. The Old Vallie struggled with born-again Vallie, but I pressed on with many tears. This was spiritual warfare!

Months later I walked into church and saw Jezebel crying. I thought about just ignoring her and just walking away. I can't ignore someone when they are clearly experiencing some trauma. I am an encourager, so I asked her what was happening. "A family member is dying," she said. God was very clear with me to pray for and with her. I understood her pain. I joined hands with her as we prayed by the stairs in church. A few weeks later I also attended the funeral service to comfort her. A month later she came to me for advice concerning a troubled family member. She took my advice and later shared the success of the relationship.

I invited God into this hard place. Do you see what God did? I had no idea what God was going to do when I surrendered it all over to Him. "I have been crucified with Christ; it is no longer I who live, but Christ lives in me. The life I now live in the body I live by faith [by adhering to, relying on, and completely trusting] in the Son of God, who loved me and gave Himself up for me" (Galatians 2:20 AMP). He allowed me to experience His mercy, grace, and love that brought restoration back into our lives.

I don't know who needed to hear my story. It is vital to know that Jezebel shows up when God is changing lives and souls are being saved and praise and worship are off the chain.

Your enemy, the devil, does not care that you love your spouse with all your heart. However, he does care that he is losing the battle of souls being delivered by the blood of Jesus. Because when Jesus comes into a person's life, that person has been released from Satan's claws. He hates us because, as spiritual leaders in the church, we choose to work alongside God. He hates us because we are servants of the Most High God and because we love Jesus. It's imperative that we know we are in a spiritual warfare. "Therefore, put on the complete armor of God, so that you will be able to [successfully] resist and stand your ground in the evil day [of danger], and having done everything [that the crisis demands], to stand firm [in your place, fully prepared, immovable, victorious]" (Ephesians 6:13 AMP).

Jezebel left our church to join another church with her family. She is attending church with her family. Look at God! I pray that she left believing that God is real and the devil is a liar. I pray my life was read as a written epistle of who God is.

What Satan meant to hurt and destroy, God revived. God rebuilt our marriage and gave us a fresh start of making new and loving memories. From this life experience, I discovered that no matter what you know, no matter what you see and hear, and no matter what you think you may know, TRUST GOD FOR EVERYTHING!

> "Trust in and rely confidently on the Lord with all your heart. And do not rely on your own insight or understanding. In all your ways know and acknowledge and recognize Him, And He will make your paths straight and smooth [removing obstacles that block your way]."
>
> Proverbs 3:5-6 AMP

> "Trust in the Lord completely, and do not rely on your own opinions. With all your heart rely on him to guide you, and he will lead you in every decision you make. Become intimate with him in whatever you do, and he will lead you wherever you go.
>
> Proverbs 3:5-6 TPT

Suburban, Not Stupid
Kim Anderson

My husband is from North Philadelphia, or as he would say, he's from Norf. I do not know if there is another neighborhood in Philly where its natives believe they are more woke in an urban sense than those from Norf. These urban gurus will consistently clown you if you're from another neighborhood, and please don't say you're from a zip code that begins with 190. See, I grew up in the suburbs, so regardless of how street-smart I am, there is this stigma on suburban girls that characterizes us as naive Stacy Dash-type clueless. But let me say this: when it comes to someone having eyes for my man, I am anything but slow.

My husband is attractive, but it's not his looks that I believe most women are attracted to; it's his swag, his confidence, and most of all, his love for the Lord. He is so real and has no pretentiousness; he has a deep passion and mission to present God in the most touchable and tangible way possible. So, here's a man's man, with nothing soft about him personally, but he has a profound sensitivity for the Lord, His Word, and His work. This is what's attractive about him and this is what I have seen many a Jezebel come and go, thinking they were going to wedge their way into his heart.

Let me also say, that it irritates me to no end when people try to disrespect my intelligence and patronize me when I sense something's not quite right. There have been several times over the years when I have noticed flirtatious behavior by a Jezebel. When I see something, I say something. However, the first reaction by my husband or anyone else who I feel I can share this Spidey sense with is to instantly dismiss it. I get it, nobody wants any drama, and trust me, I am the most drama-free person there is, but I'm suburban, not stupid. I don't like being played or placated. And those who are supposed to care about their pastor and his marriage and family definitely should not be coddling a Jezebel because they have grown a liking to them; to me that's the most disrespectful Judas in the church. But I'm here to talk about Jezebel, so let me stay on task. Anyway, there are three types of Jezebels I've encountered over the last twenty years that I'd like to warn all my ladies about. You have your Fan Girl Jezebel who's like a Pastor Groupie, you have your Damsel in Distress Jezebel, who's broken and vulnerable and just desperately needs her pastor, and finally, you have your Joe Familiar Jezebel who walked in yesterday but acts like they've known your husband for years.

I remember the Fan Girl Jezebel started visiting our church mostly on special occasions. There was nothing particularly special about her, but she found a way to stand out. Sometimes it was her overwhelming exaggerated appreciation for the preached Word. If I heard Jezebels over the years say it once, I heard it a thousand times. "Oh, Pastor, I don't know how you know what's going on in my life, but you were speaking directly to me today." And I'm standing there listening to her, and in my own head, I'm thinking like, "Oh was he now?" Jezebel's desire is to make my husband feel like he is so spiritually in tune with her; it's just unbelievable. Jezebel would go as far as to say in her presumably joking yet inappropriate way, "Do you have cameras in my house?"

Now, I know without a doubt my husband was not interested in this woman at all, but what man does not like their ego stroked? My husband would not cater to her advances, but he would flippantly dismiss them as harmless and tell me not to trip about it. See, it's so trifling to see a woman pay your husband so much attention, and they don't even speak to you. This woman did her best to avoid me at all costs. She knew she was guilty of lusting after my man, and I truly believe in her mind she thought she was a threat to our marriage. Look here, I might be suburban, but I'm not stupid. I'm not just watching her physically, but I'm daily rebuking that Jezebel spirit and praying her hind parts right out of those doors. In a short period of time, my husband did sense this woman was up to something, and he shared that with his security and his accountability crew, and poof, Fan Girl was gone as fast as her fast little self, came.

I've seen the Fan Girl type of Jezebel several times over the last two decades, but let me tell you about Miss Damsel in Distress, Jezebel. This is the one who is struggling with all of life and the only one who can save them is? You guessed it—Pastor. Now my husband does not meet with women alone and he does not counsel women. Therefore, these women have to work really hard and get pretty creative to get my husband to hear their issues. But believe it or not, they are willing to jump through the hoops to do so. My husband is the type of pastor who stands in the back of the sanctuary at the door following worship service to greet everyone as they leave the church. Well, this is where Jezebel tried to create a moment between her and my husband. She did not just want a hug or a greeting upon leaving. She wanted to ask him for a special prayer. She desperately needed his advice and now he was on the spot, and although the room was crowded, he had to stop everything to give her this moment.

If this happened one time and I had a problem with it, I could understand someone saying, "Kim, you may be a little insecure or overreacting," but what do you do when this scene is repeated continuously? When she wants to start a conversation every week with your husband. Do you request your husband dismiss her and tell her now is not the time? Truthfully, there is literally no other time when he will dialogue with her, and she knows this. Do I say something to her, which I know the moment I do, that Jezebel spirit in her will elevate this thing to bring confusion and chaos into our lives and ministry? Well, I'll tell you what I did. I shared my concerns with my husband, and I shared my concerns with my God. God assured me that He had removed the enemies from our lives before and He would do it again. I did not let this Jezebel get a foothold in our home and God made sure she did not get a foothold in our church. Ladies, if you are reading this, listen to me because I cannot say this enough: spiritual weapons must be used in spiritual battles if you want spiritual results. Do not allow your insecure flesh to make these scenarios about you. The enemy is on the prowl, but we are more than conquerors through Him who love us.

The final type of Jezebel I want to share about is the Joe Familiar Jezebel. This is the type of woman who intentionally gets close to you in order to get even closer to your husband. I thank God I have never experienced this type of Jezebel. However, her kind has been brought to my attention by other pastors' wives. I have heard some stories, and I have definitely heeded the warnings of those who are too friendly and self-inviting into your lives. I was informed these Joe Familiar Jezebels could even use their spiritual mentoring of your children at church as an opportunity to get into your home. It's so ridiculous. Sometimes you can listen to this type of activity and ask yourself, "Are we talking about the church or an Oprah Winfrey Soap Opera?" Even as I write this, I'm thinking of how many men have fallen for one of these women sent by the enemy to destroy their homes and disrupt their houses of worship. I would venture to say the majority of these pastors were not seeking an affair, but they also were not wearing the full armor of God to protect themselves from it. To my sisters, I hope this entry puts some flesh on these mystical women who slither their way into our churches and attempt to enter into our homes.

Remember, ladies, we must be alert and of sober mind, so we can recognize these roaring lions prowling around. Because it's one thing they all need to know: I may be suburban, but I'm not stupid.

Jezebel Summary
Christine O. James

A Closing Point of View:

I have lost count of how many times we have encountered Jezebels in our community. This divisive spirit has shown up so often that I usually recognize it coming through the door. The devil doesn't have many new tricks, so the tools that Jezebel uses generally show up pretty quickly. Sometimes it's the damsel in distress, other times it's arrogant pride and still other times it's the exceedingly helpful person who seems to have all of the things you or your spouse need or desire.

The challenging thing about this spirit is that because it shows up within a human, we have to find a way to love the human but prayerfully confront the spirit. My husband has a saying that "Some battles have to be fought with our hands tied behind our backs." Whew, that's sometimes easier said than done. Another visual for me comes from the movie *Gladiator*. When the men were at the front line of the battle, ready to fight, Maximus, the leader of the soldiers, said, "Hold, hold...hold the line. Stay with me!" I believe that is what the Spirit of God often says to me when I encounter the Jezebel spirit. Just because we recognize that there is something going on in the person that is opposite to the works of God does not mean that we should address the issue right away. We must hold the line and stay with God. Do not attempt to fight any battle that God has not prepared you for or asked you to fight.

Jezebel often shows up when we have gone through either a great victory or a great loss. It shows up in extremes. After great highs or lows, we need a rest, a retreat. That is often when manipulation and deception begin. Jezebel thrives on discouragement, on those times when we feel that we have nothing left to give. The ultimate goal is to make us doubt the power of God at work in our lives.

We must beware of what I call, "discouragement sleep"; those times when you are not necessarily sleeping because you are tired, but rather sleeping because you have lost hope. When Jezebel threatened Elijah, he went and lay down under a bush. God sent an angel to tell him to get up and eat so he would be able to make the journey ahead of him. We, too, must trust the Lord to help us get up. We must get up and eat so that we would have the strength to do all that God has assigned for us to do. Go forth, mighty warrior! You've got this!

Scriptures for Prayerful Reflection:

There is nothing concealed that will not be disclosed, or hidden that will not be made known. What you have said in the dark will be heard in the daylight, and what you have whispered in the ear in the inner rooms will be proclaimed from the roofs.
~ Luke 12:2-3 NIV

Though the mountains be shaken
and the hills be removed,
yet my unfailing love for you will not be shaken
nor my covenant of peace be removed,"
says the Lord, who has compassion on you.
~ Isaiah 54:10 NIV

> Love is patient, love is kind. It does not envy, it does not boast, it is not proud. It does not dishonor others, it is not self-seeking, it is not easily angered, it keeps no record of wrongs. Love does not delight in evil but rejoices with the truth. It always protects, always trusts, always hopes, always perseveres.
> ~ 1 Corinthians 13:4-7 NIV

Let's Pray Together:

Jesus, when you saw the crowds, harassed and helpless, you were moved with compassion. Help us, Lord, to do the same. People come into our churches with complex issues that can be difficult to navigate. Help us, Lord, to be wise as serpents, and gentle as doves. Give us wisdom and insight as to how to walk with those you bring into our communities in a way that brings you glory. Please fill us again with your Spirit so that we can walk in your unfailing love. Amen.

JOY
Contributors

Introduction
Dr. Larry L. Anderson Jr.

The Search for Joy
Tirzah L. Fontell

Despite My Losses, I Still Have Joy
Sharon E. Burton

Joy for the Journey
Shirley A. Wilson

The Joy of Serving
Telisha Acklin

Joy Summary
Christine O. James

Introduction
Dr. Larry L Anderson Jr.

If one were to have joy defined by the Merriam-Webster dictionary, it would sound like this: *the emotion evoked by well-being, success, or good fortune or by the prospect of possessing what one desires.* However, if joy were to be defined by Scripture, it would sound more like this, "Consider it pure joy, my brothers and sisters, whenever you face trials of many kinds, because you know that the testing of your faith produces perseverance. Let perseverance finish its work so that you may be mature and complete, not lacking anything" (James 1:2-4 NIV).

To consider something in a joyful manner means you are deciding to have a godly perspective on your worldly matters. There is no way any woman can possess the dictionary definition of joy when they're repeatedly jilted, betrayed by Judas, constantly facing judgment, dealing with jealousy, and worrying about little old Jezebel over there eyeballing her man, all while possessing the Webster's definition of joy. But you can go through all of this and still have biblical joy. The joyous attitude that recognizes each day as holy to our Lord, and the joy of the Lord is your strength.

I know it is easier to define joy and quote Scriptures concerning joy than it is to sometimes possess joy but:

I'm reminded of Mary, the mother of Jesus, whose entire life was uprooted as a teenage girl and changed. She had to face judgment concerning her pregnancy out of wedlock, which could have led to a divorce or stoning. However, due to her understanding that her situation was according to the plans of God, she offers a song of praise communicating how her soul magnifies the Lord, and her spirit rejoices in her God and Savior (Luke 1:47 ESV).

I'm reminded of Hagar, who had to feel jilted after being a servant to Sarah. Once so close and like family, chose by Sarah to sleep with Abraham and be a surrogate mother to a child for them. Then Hagar was mistreated and ultimately sent away from the family. She was a single mother with no security, no future, and no idea if she would live or die. However, because of her blessed encounter with the Lord, she began to use a new name for Him. Hagar called Him *The God Who Sees Me*. Recognizing that in spite of where she was or what she was going through, God still saw her and cared for her.

I'm reminded of Esther, who had to battle her own Judas in the form of Haman to save her people. As a first lady chosen based on her looks versus her brains or character, she was placed in a seemingly no-win situation. However, after recognizing the significance of her placement in God's kingdom, she risked her own position in her human kingdom for such a time as this.

I'm reminded of Rachel, who had to view her sister as a Jezebel because although Jacob was fooled into sleeping with her sister Leah, Rachel was fully aware of the deception she was involved in. Rachel being barren and seeing her sister have children with the man who loved her almost more than life itself had to make her not only jealous but insecure and desperate. But she still cried out to the Lord, recognizing His sovereignty over her childbearing. She praised the Lord when she was able to conceive a child and viewed Joseph's birth as a victory in the Lord. Finally, she even told Jacob to follow the voice of the Lord when he needed to make the most critical decision concerning their family's relocation.

None of these women were perfect, nor did they find themselves in perfect situations, but the one thing they all had in common, as with our pastors' wives who contributed to this book, is a perfect God. A God who sees the people and the circumstances they find themselves in and will reward them accordingly. The truth is, that the home of the pastor needs to be a place of shalom. However, our enemy, the devil, desires the exact opposite. To introduce conflict and chaos in a pastor's home is a huge win for Satan. To get a man and his wife to begin pointing fingers and assigning blame is a win. To tempt someone to question their relationship with one another and, worse, how to slant God's Word in their favor in their situation is a recipe for disaster, but it's exactly what the devil wants.

Pastors, the last thing you want in life is to minister to everyone in your congregation and neglect your first ministry, which is your wife. There are few moments that can feel more hypocritical in the life of a neglected pastor's wife than the celebration of the pastor's anniversary. This is an event where everyone shares such wonderful testimonies about their husband's ministry with them, while ironically, his wife has tears in her eyes and wishes she had received a percentage of that attention. As much as you may believe you do all you do for everyone else, your wife and family need the same care and tenderness you gave to others. God has called you. Please remember that one of the number one qualifications of being able to do for them is that you are already doing so for those in your own household. So, Pastor, please love that woman and cover those children, because in the end, many members may remember the memories you shared with them, but at home, they will always remember the memories you were missing from.

First ladies, I have learned a lot by writing this book. I have wept, repented, and sought the face of God on your behalf. I know this book will not change the world, but I do pray it brings some level of validation of your voice and recognizes the call you, women, have on your lives. I will always advocate for you, and I pray the church will recognize the neglect, the stigmas, and the stereotypes placed upon you all. I pray you all are able to find trust and solidarity with other pastors' wives. I pray the spiritual warfare of divide and conquer will be broken and overcome by the Holy Spirit within you all. Finally, I encourage you to recite, meditate, and pray on Psalm 16:11 in your moments of trial and despair. "You make known to me the path of life; you will fill me with joy in your presence, with eternal pleasures at your right hand."

Amen!

The Search for Joy
Tizrah L. Fontell

Dear Diary, I have been a pastor's wife for 18 years and almost 16 years as a senior pastor's wife, or first lady, as some call us. When I think back, it was simpler being the wife of a youth pastor. It was simpler because the demands were different, or shall I say less. I had a different kind of joy then because, well, ministry was fun. My husband worked 9 to 5. He was the youth pastor, not the senior pastor at that time. We were still busy with ministry, teaching the youth, and planning events, but the mental and emotional responsibility was different. Lighter.

As the wife of a senior pastor, I still have joy, but it is different. When my husband shared he felt God calling him into full-time ministry, I did not respond with excitement but with fear. I did not want to be a senior pastor's wife! What would this mean for us as a couple? I know of ministry couples who did not make it because the adjustment was too hard. I did not want to be a hindrance to God's call on his life either, but my immediate reaction was not joy! Of course, I wanted to support him, but what about me? How was our quality of life going to be affected?

So many thoughts ran through my mind. I was very selfish in my time with him and still can be at times, but I learned through the years I must navigate those feelings when they arise. I knew I did not want to lose what we had or let the church become all-consuming. In the beginning years, it was hard. There were many nights when he had so many late meetings that kept him away from home. I began to feel like what was happening here! This could not be God's plan for our life. It was hard to find joy because the journey was starting to feel lonely quickly. He was busy, and I was trying to figure out how I was going to adjust. I started reflecting on when I said I did not want to be a hindrance and what that would look like. He was so busy most of the time or tired from trying to assimilate into this new life we had. So, in this new life I was not completely ready for, I needed to seek what I found joyful.

I do know that working outside the church has been a beneficial outlet as it does help alleviate some of the stressors associated with the role of the pastor's wife. After a year or so of being at Calvary, I did try what some might call the traditional path of some first ladies, which is leading the women's ministry. I did not find joy in that. It was just not my lane. I decided to work with the praise dance ministry, which I loved! I enjoyed sharing what I learned from my many years of dancing with The Philadelphia Civic Ballet Company, Pennsylvania Ballet Company, Philadanco, JUBA, and Alvin Ailey. I was sharing that training with those who wanted to dance for the Lord! Listening to music that ministered to me and putting choreography to the song was exhilarating! I was in my happy place! I was excited to come to practice on Saturday morning and see those young ladies and women ready to learn some new choreography so they could minister to the congregation and the Lord through dance on a Sunday. I can hear a song today, and if it ministers to me, movements to it start brewing in my mind.

I am currently serving in the new discipleship ministry, and what brings me joy is seeing new souls come to Christ and their lives changed as they begin their journey in Christ. It is so refreshing to see the zeal of babes in Christ and to come alongside them on their journey. I also believe that feeding my personal joys outside my duties as a pastor's wife is vitally important. With the demands that come from my husband being a senior pastor, spontaneity in the things we were used to doing together can be stifled. So as not to become disheartened because of the demands of the pastorate, a wise friend told me that sometimes we must create our own joy. I find joy in spending time with my grandchildren. Shopping. I love window shopping; I find it very therapeutic. I have recently taken up collecting niche perfumes. I have always loved fragrances, but when COVID-19 had us shut in, I began learning about perfume houses. This may seem frivolous, but I am sharing what brings me joy in my journey as a pastor's wife. However, on the days when this journey seems all-consuming, there are more of those days than I care for.

On many occasions, there have been meetings, member visits, sermons, and Bible study preps that have often caused me to adjust our plans. To keep my joy from waning, I turn to listening to praise and worship music, meditating on how God loves me in the Word, and just resting at His feet. In my journey as pastor's wife, in the Black churches I know, first ladies have led or lead the women's ministry and done it well! Dr. Melissa Jones of The Bible Way Baptist Church. First Lady Patricia Richardson of The Stronghold Baptist Church. It was suggested when I came to Calvary Christian Church, known as Calvary Baptist Church at that time, that I lead the women's ministry. I accepted, but it did not bring me joy, so I stepped down.

However, as stated earlier, I am part of the new discipleship ministry. I love being part of the journey when a new soul comes to Christ! I am even getting my feet wet with the communications ministry in getting our church's social media presence out there. That brings me joy as I am learning to hone skills in the social media world that is being used to draw attention to Jesus Christ! While I may not be an upfront pastor's wife, I have found my joy in the places where I can serve the King!

Despite My Losses, I Still Have Joy
Sharon F. Burton

Dear Diary, There have been times in my life, and in ministry, when I experienced a disconnect. Not from the Lord, but from the ministry itself. I say this from my perspective as a former pastor's wife. Although it has always been my heart's desire to be together as one in ministry, I was not afforded this luxury.

Over the past 40-plus years, I have met a plethora of pastors and their wives whom I greatly admire. Their ministries as a couple are vibrant and flourishing. Even their children excelled in the ways of God and added to their picture-perfect testimonies for all to see. Being a realist, I am fully cognizant of the fact that there is no perfect scenario, but I must admit there are those who seem to have a connectedness. These ministry couples not only walk together as one but acknowledge, appreciate, and affirm what each brings to the table. Puzzled, I asked myself, "Why did that not happen to me?"

I purposed as God purposed for my life to be the best wife anyone could be. Not all was unbearable down through the years, but I was never expected to be unaccepted or unable to exercise the gifts God gave to me.

There was a very present sense of a lack of cohesiveness, which had a direct impact on our ability to effectively minister. This permeated and prevailed throughout the life of the family and the pastoral ministry. This unfortunate lack of oneness was reflected in our joint testimony.

Why or what caused this lack of oneness? Initially, it at times appears that ministry begins on an even keel. However, somewhere along the way, fear, doubt, anxiety, and self, get in the way. Some spouses begin to see their partners as unnecessary or even a threat. Why is there a rivalry or rift between two who are called to be co-laborers? Is there a need to compete with or against the other? Where did the joy of serving Jesus leave the hearts of man? Personally, I have been appalled at these interruptions in service. Is it perhaps that our service as servants is no longer unto God? At what point does a partner lack appreciation, reverence, or recognition of their ministry partner?

Who knew that I would feel cast down and forsaken? All I ever wanted was to experience the joy of ministry alongside my husband-pastor. However, I was constantly and purposely left out, counted as not worthy to be a co-laborer. At best, I was a necessary "evil" who was expected to keep a certain posture, face, and attitude. In other words, play a part—silently! I experienced the hurt of being undervalued, irrelevant, ignored, and unwanted. What I have come to know is that in playing the part silently, I did myself a disservice. God was not pleased!

God's Word lets us know that in this life, we will have tribulation. I recognize that I am not above the law or exempt, but through it all, God has been good to me! Despite my circumstances and my faults and failures, the Lord continues to bless and favor me! Hallelujah!

Just sharing the above brings back the reality of loss. I never would have imagined the loss of a marriage, loss of a pastoral ministry, loss of a community and congregation, and a loss of self in the process. But thanks be unto God! *Despite my losses, I still have joy!* It's the joy of my salvation and present status of life that encourages me to continue, faith over fear. In fact, my life is now forever changed! Counting my blessings through it all confirms that this experience (my past) was the catalyst to propel me into a deeper and more committed relationship with Christ. No longer do I depend on or rely on a person, place, or thing. I recognize that all that I am or ever hope to be is in Christ. It is truly no longer me but Christ who lives in me! For this, I give God all the praise and all the honor, and I surrender anew my life to be a channel of blessing.

Who knew that at this juncture of my life, I would be here? Separated from my home, my marriage, and my former way of living? BUT GOD! His plan prevails, and I am in awe of His favor over my life. I have a newfound joy, and YES, it is unspeakable! Without a doubt, the world did not, and cannot, give this joy to me, and surely it cannot take it away! I'm no worse for the wear, but better because of it. I am more than a conqueror through Him who loves me!

So, guess what has transpired since? Open doors!! Effectual and open doors of ministry. I am overjoyed by the fact that God chooses to use me as His vessel. He has opened my vista and ushered in freedom to first recap and reacquaint myself with the person I almost lost along the way—me! I found out I am resilient and able to have gifts that were once stifled; I am being introduced to new open doors. God has opened windows by which He steadily pours out blessings in my life. I am one of His grateful and thankful children.

Truly, I have found that your gifts will make room for you. Where I once felt there was "no room," I now am released to flow in my giftings and calling. Upon uniting with my new church home, I was immediately asked to join in a collaborative partnership. I am blessed to work alongside this man of God (who I now know to be a dearly beloved brother and friend in Christ). We are leaders of the new members ministry. Little did I know that this was God performing a miracle and that I would be connected to a true and dear friend who remains. Finally, I get to work with the same commitment, energy, and dedication to the

Lord with someone who recognizes my worth. We are honored to work together for the cause of Christ. As my brother and friend would say, "The rest remains to be seen."

At present, I have been invited to join the intercessory prayer and women's ministries. Over the last two years, I have been invited to be a guest speaker at various conferences. I continue my biblical studies as a student of continuing education at the Church, and I am a regular devotional speaker as part of a Christian radio broadcast known as *From the Heart of His Majesty's Throne*. I provide a message of encouragement to God's people. I never imagined any of this for my life, and now I'm privileged and honored to participate in writing my thoughts for this book!

To God be the glory. GREAT things He has done! "I get joy when I think about what He's done for me" is not just the words to a song; it is the song to my life! I know full well that my Father loves me, He keeps me, He provides for me and He will always take care of me. His joy gives me peace, rest, and the confidence I need so that "I can do all things through Christ which strengthens me" (Philippians 4:13 NKJV) is my life verse.

God is yet revealing, nurturing, and cultivating my life. I am assured of His divine intent for me, and rest in His plan; the plan that I read in Jeremiah 29:11-14 KJV: "For I know the thoughts that I think toward you, saith the LORD, thoughts of peace, and not of evil, to give you an expected end. Then shall ye call upon me, and ye shall go and pray unto me, and I will hearken unto you. And ye shall seek me, and find *me* when ye shall search for me with all your heart." There is a path of continued service I must travel, and I'm grateful to know He will lead and guide me in the way of truth and paths of righteousness.

The joy I have is preparing me for the rest of my journey. Although adversity and offenses may come, I will rest in the fact that I am covered by His blood and that nothing shall separate me from His love.

Everything must and will work together for my good and God's glory. Shifting gears, I have the blessed assurance that I can depend on God.

Joy brings excitement, and I am excited to see what He has in store for me. I'm blessed with health and strength for each day I have a loving relationship with my three adult children and my adorable grandchildren, and I'm free; praise the Lord, I'm free! Learning to accept what God says I am, I embrace Psalm 139:14 KJV, "I will praise thee; for I am fearfully and wonderfully made: marvelous are thy works; and that my soul knoweth right well" to be my best and authentic self and to do what is assigned to my hand.

Despite my losses, I still have joy!

Joy for the Journey
Shirley A. Wilson

Dear Diary, As the daughter of a bi-vocational Baptist pastor, I grew up in the church. I watched my mother enthusiastically serve as a very personable, hands-on partner alongside her pastor-husband. Times were different back then. The polished, professional first lady did not yet exist, and neither did the term. Make no mistake, there were a few general expectations in place, the main one being that women, even the pastor's wife, were to be seen and not really heard.

Mom didn't have a special seat in the sanctuary. In fact, she rarely sat at all. Instead, she sang in the choir, ushered, was the worship leader for annual days, baked cakes for repasts, cleaned up after the dinners, taught Sunday school, directed the Christmas play, visited with the older sisters she viewed as mentors and more. Mom genuinely loved the people of our small congregation, and they loved her. She gave her heart and soul into all she did for the church and brought us along in the process. As much as she enjoyed church work, she also endured the wrath of disgruntled members, rumors, surprise betrayals and the subsequent ecclesiastical coup d'état while defending her husband's biblical stance, which ultimately ended in the pastor's resignation from the church. We had to leave the church she had grown to love.

She was Sister Wilson, wife, mother of five, full-time employee and a busy pastor's wife. Her example, coupled with an authentic encounter with Jesus as a teenage girl, generally prepared me for church ministry life, or so I thought. Nothing could be further from the truth.

Reflecting on our 38 married years of pastoral ministry, I have discovered just how unique it all is. After all, the pastorate is both an occupation and a calling. As an occupation, he is compensated to perform. As a calling, he was created to perform. Like most wives, I desire to support my husband in both aspects. Did you ever notice that a pastor's wife is the only spouse automatically expected, even required, to work directly alongside her husband? Think about it. A dentist's wife doesn't pull teeth; neither is a lawyer's wife expected to practice law; however, the pastor's wife is expected to be a jack of all ministry trades. Besides being able to sing and possibly play the piano, she is expected to be beautiful and fashionably dressed (my mother loved hats), able to speak and teach the Word of God, as well as to utter meaningful words of encouragement at the appropriate time.

For many clergy couples, the struggle comes when the pastor and wife are not on one accord regarding her role and responsibilities at the church. Admittedly, most of us enjoy the perks that come with this role. Perks like fancy clothes, preferential seating, dinners, gifts, recognition, respect, trips, banquets, etc. Concurrently, I don't know of any pastor's wife who has been able to totally avoid the issue of frustration, rejection, stress, and even betrayal inherent in our ministry role. The blurred line between marriage and ministry, clergy and congregation, servant and the served, our families and the faithful, can create a breeding ground of internal resentment and marital discord. Can I get a witness?

In addition to the occupational hazards threatening pastoral marriage and home, there is life. We are not exempt from the vicissitudes of life in any way just because we're married to a pastor. Nod to Langston Hughes, "Life for me ain't been no crystal stair." For all of our marriage,

I've suffered from chronic illness. Crohn's disease invaded our lives from the start. Later came kidney disease, renal failure, and the life sentence of dialysis; I can't count the resulting hospitalizations, procedures, and surgeries preventing me from attending church services and enjoying major events while I attempted to support from the hospital bed or home. I've missed out on exciting opportunities such as yearly mission trips to Zambia, Africa, India or Nepal. I never wanted my poor health to interfere with his ministry career or to thrust him into the caretaker role. Such is life.

On January 4, 2011, we got the call that no parents want to receive. Our youngest son, Michael J. Wilson, had been killed in a bridge construction accident. He was 20 years old. Wait a minute. Why would the God we so faithfully served steal our son from us? Instantly, we had to live life with a deep hole in our hearts. The fishbowl aspect of ministry laid us bare in our weakest hour. How do we carry such grief and emptiness? The silence was deafening. After all, who really knows how to minister to the pastor and his family? Sure, we received calls, food, and visits for which we were very thankful. We knew Michael's village was also grieving, but once the services were over, very few people spoke of our tragedy or of our amazing son again. It was an awkward situation, causing people to walk and talk on eggshells when in our presence. I got the sense that people were afraid to mention it because they did not want to cause more pain for us. I think people interpreted our stoicism as innate strength as opposed to our being humanly numb, frozen in the experience, operating like dutiful robots. We clung to each other, attempting to navigate life in our new normal, now replete with emptiness and heaviness of heart. Without the supernatural strength of our God in us gently forcing us back into reality, we would not be capable of moving forward. Believe me! We know it was God who kept us and continues to keep us.

Time and space do not permit me to discuss aging, ill parents, the death of his lovely parents, and my beautiful mother. Amid it all, I have continued working a full-time job as a teacher for the past 36 years. Both of us were working hard to financially maintain and sacrifice for our personal and ministry goals. There is much in my life over which I have no control, pastor's wife or not. One thing I do have control over is how I respond to what happens in my personal life, my marriage, family, and ministry. At the center of it all is my personal relationship with God through Jesus Christ. Developing and maintaining a personal, authentic, spiritual connection with Him changes my selfish perspective. As God the Holy Spirit works in me, coupled with grace, and God's enabling power, I am strengthened despite life crisis. In my weakness, His strength is at its best! No time for pity parties over here.

I view my pastor's wife's role as a calling in that God Himself ordained and orchestrated our union. Without that, we could not work in concert for the Kingdom. I realize that people are watching us, him and me. This is what helps me to love and serve God's people like my mother did all those years ago.

The foundation of it all—home, church, life—is joy. A byproduct of the Spirit, joy is the state of godly contentment and well-being despite circumstances. Despite the external problems at home, physical/emotional turmoil, crisis of faith, rumors, etc., I make an internal choice to rejoice. As Nehemiah, leader of Israel's wall rebuilding project, declared, "... for the joy of the Lord is your strength" (Nehemiah 8:10 NIV). Joy allows me to live above the circumstances in spite of trials. In fact, joy propels me onward and upward away from typical, natural, expected perspectives to supernatural attitudes and actions.

Ministry life is a roller coaster of emotions: Starting a church from scratch in your living room is scary. When your husband leaves a full-time secular job for full-time pastoring you're the only one with a steady salary and benefits. When both, church attendance and offering are low, and those you love leave the church for unknown reasons. When people look to you to share, and even ease their sorrow and pain during death and sickness, only joy will sustain and re-energize you for tasks you didn't know you were capable of doing.

My decision to embrace joy allows me to smile/laugh when I should be crying, to run when nobody/nothing is chasing me, and to press onward and upward when circumstances are pushing me back. Not sure what life will bring or what my health challenges will require in the future, whether serving as a part of the 9-member core group that planted our 26-year-old church, women's ministry director, children's ministry teacher, or praise team/choir singer, I'll continue to serve as my pastor-husband needs and God allows.

That's my journey, and I view it as a joyful one. The words of our tradition are appropriate right about now, for they echo what's in my heart:

> This joy I have
>
> The world didn't give it to me
>
> The world didn't give it
>
> The world can't take it away!

The Joy of Serving
Telisha Acklin

Dear Diary, The joy in serving as a first lady embracing the role of a pastor's wife is a journey filled with profound joy despite the demanding and occasionally lonely aspects. The delight arises not from personal accomplishments but from fulfilling one's purpose within God's plan for His people. Joy, defined as a feeling of great pleasure and happiness, often eludes us in the midst of ministry work and its associated stresses. However, it is essential to find immense satisfaction in sowing seeds that cultivate a deeper connection with Christ in the lives of those we serve. The joy in serving emerges not only from what we do but from witnessing the transformation in the lives of others touched by God's grace.

Amidst the challenges, it's easy to overlook the growth within our families. Our children may be developing their own love for the Lord, and our husbands may be deepening their affection for us through their study of the Word. In the hustle and bustle, we may feel neglected and lose sight of the joy in the moments our husbands carve out for us. It becomes crucial to pause and reflect on the progress made over the years in our personal walks with God, our families, and our congregations. Reflecting on our own experiences, we find joy in witnessing our youngest son's evolution from a tentative 10-year-old drummer to a passionate musician, drawing people to church to feel God's presence. I beam with pride when I see him feel God's presence and share with his sisters that their brother has left the building. Teasing that he has elevated and is sitting on the cusp of heaven with his praise.

Celebrating our oldest son's marriage, we hear his best man and college roommate share that he prayed for a friend he could look up to and who loved the Lord. He stated he got everything and more from those prayers. That our son was truly a lover of Christ and set many examples that kept them going in the right direction. As parents, the gratitude expressed by the best man resonated deeply and is confirmation that God's promise is true. It was a precious gift to hear a testimony about our son. Knowing that God guided us to raise a young man who wasn't afraid to show his love for Christ and live that in front of his college peers. These moments, shaped by our own walks with Christ, verbal expressions, and intentions to serve, bring great joy.

Maintaining joy in our hearts, even during challenging circumstances, enables God to move mountains and infuses us with renewed vigor for ministry. It opens unforeseen opportunities and fosters personal growth. Our focus shifts from current challenges to future outcomes, strengthening our resolve to serve joyfully. As the ministry evolves and transforms, we find enduring joy in knowing that God's hands guide us. It's a reminder that the joy of the Lord becomes our strength in navigating the various seasons of ministry. Whether celebrating births, witnessing unions, guiding individuals toward Christ, or experiencing miracles, the joy derived from our husbands' preached words, and even bidding farewell to those who meet Jesus on the other side, is enough to sustain us. It's crucial to remember that everything we endure as first ladies contributes to the greater good, allowing us to rest peacefully, knowing we walk in His purpose.

Regardless of whether one serves visibly or supports behind the scenes, there is joy in every form of service. God recognizes and appreciates our contributions, so take pride and joy in whatever role He has entrusted you with as a first lady. In times when the spotlight may not be on you, where your service is more behind the scenes, it's essential to acknowledge that your role alongside your husband is significant. God sees your dedication and is pleased with your support in the ministry.

Take pride and joy in the unique way He has appointed you as a first lady. This joy isn't contingent upon public recognition but stems from the knowledge that your service aligns with God's plan. As a supportive force beside your husband, your impact ripples through the lives of those you touch. Your role, whether visible or unseen, plays a vital part in the cohesive functioning of the ministry. Consider the joy derived from the relationships cultivated, the prayers whispered and the encouragement offered to those who may never stand in the pulpit. Your service shapes a nurturing and welcoming environment within the church, contributing to its spiritual growth. Every act of kindness, every moment of empathy, and every word of encouragement you provide carries profound significance.

While the demands of this role may be overwhelming at times, remember that joy is not just an outcome; it's a companion on the journey. Find joy in the small victories, the moments of connection, and the knowledge that your service, however discreet, is impactful in the grand tapestry of God's plan.

In those instances when loneliness creeps in or when the challenges seem insurmountable, hold on to the joy found in the quiet moments of reflection and prayer. Your dedication, even when unnoticed, is seen by the One who matters most. Trust that God is weaving a beautiful story through your life, one that contributes to the flourishing of His Kingdom. As first ladies, our service is a testament to our commitment to God, our husbands, and the congregation. Let the joy in serving be your compass, guiding you through the tough times and illuminating the path ahead. Whether you find yourself at the forefront or working diligently behind the scenes, know that your service matters and the joy derived from it is a reflection of God's grace working through you. Embrace the joy that comes from a life dedicated to God's purpose, relish the shared moments of growth and transformation, and rest in the assurance that your service, no matter how understated, is a vital component of the divine narrative unfolding in the lives of those you serve.

As first ladies, we cultivate a steadfast focus on joy and discern God's glory by nurturing a consistent and personal relationship with God through prayer, and Scripture study provides a source of strength and renewal. Having a relationship with him individually sustains me in times of need. It keeps me grounded in His love for me versus focusing on the moments of discouragement. We must create and foster relationships with fellow first ladies, trusted friends, and family members that allow for shared experiences and encouragement. Building connections with those who understand the unique challenges of this role provides a space for shared wisdom and mutual support. There's nothing like a good girl's time and laughter when you get together or just talk on the phone to be poured into and your concerns are met with a like-minded individual saying everything is going to be alright.

Lastly, maintaining a perspective centered on the eternal impact of their service reinforces the intrinsic joy found in living out God's purpose. Remember that the challenges with husbands, children, and church dynamics are temporary, while God's favor and the enduring joy He provides remain constant, helping us navigate through difficulties without losing sight of the bigger picture. Always remember your joy is in the Lord! For He cares for you and will continuously give you the desires of your heart when you stay focused on His purpose and not your circumstance. So never lose sight of who you are and who you are in your service to your husband and the church! It is always a great joy to serve Christ in the capacity of first lady

Joy Summary
Christine O. James

A Closing Point of View:

People just want to feel better. Always in search of what will make them happy. It is common for people to leave churches, jobs, and even their families because they are simply not happy. Unfortunately, happiness, because it is based on happenstance, or a given set of circumstances in our lives, is only temporary. Like taking a drug to feel better, once it wears off, the root cause of the problem will come rushing back.

Unlike happiness, joy is an enduring sense of contentment and peace. It stems from an uncluttered heart and soul. When we try to take on the world, feeling like our success or failure depends upon us, we set ourselves up for deep disappointment. It wasn't until I learned to press into the presence of the Lord, to worship Him and not my capacity to do a given thing, that my life completely changed.

Worship is the stimulant of joy. It's like embers in a fireplace. If you stoke the embers, the dry wood on top will eventually be set ablaze. Worship answers all of the taunting questions that seek to rob us of our joy. When we see God properly, we understand his intentions and promises toward us. The best things in life can only be perceived in his presence, where there is fullness of joy. As we worship, joy acts as a divine windshield wiper that clears away anything that could potentially cloud our judgment about God's great love for us. We all have a decision to make each day to either do things or purchase things to try to make ourselves happy, which is often fleeting, or to choose joy, soul-sustaining joy in his presence. Praying joy for you today.

Scriptures for Prayerful Reflection:

Nehemiah said, "Go and enjoy choice food and sweet drinks, and send some to those who have nothing prepared. This day is holy to our Lord. Do not grieve, for the joy of the Lord is your strength."
~ Nehemiah 8:10 NIV

You make known to me the path of life;
you will fill me with joy in your presence,
with eternal pleasures at your right hand.
~ Psalm 16:11 NIV

Though you have not seen him, you love him; and even though you do not see him now, you believe in him and are filled with an inexpressible and glorious joy, for you are receiving the end result of your faith, the salvation of your souls.
~ 1 Peter 1:8-9 NIV

Let's Pray Together:

Lord, we are so grateful for your presence. Your presence brings joy, and your joy brings about our strength. Thank you for not leaving us to figure things out for ourselves. You have not left us to our own imaginations and creativity; rather, your Holy Spirit leads us right back to your heart, to lead and guide us into all truth. God, we will choose you and your joy again and again. Because of your son Jesus, Amen.

A Question

Thank You. Thank You. Thank You for reading *The Pastors' Wives' Diaries*! I hope you were enlightened and encouraged as you read. I hope you saw, in spite of the many challenges these women faced, they continued to persevere in being the helpers the Lord has called them to be. I hope you can feel my heart in penning this apology to not only my wife but to pastors' wives all over the world.

My question is, do you believe the stories shared from these women's hearts are valuable and important to gain an understanding of them and to foster greater relationships within the pastoral family and the church? If you answered yes, I would like to invite you to become an ambassador for the Diaries Series. What does an ambassador do? I'm glad you asked. I would ask that you pray for these women. I would also ask that you share this book with your family and friends. Would you please post it on your social media platforms? There is no greater way to let people know something is of value than to hear it from someone they know and trust, and that someone is you. Finally,

I would love it if you would consider visiting Amazon and leaving a review, as I truly want to hear what you think of this book.

Serving Together,

Larry L. Anderson Jr.

Other Works

The PASTORS' DIARIES: An Intimate Look Behind the Pulpit, released July 2022 through WestBow Press.

http://drlarrylandersonjr.com

ASK ME WHY I'M NOT IN CHURCH: A Call for The Church to Get Out of The Building, released June 2019 through WestBow Press.

http://drlarrylandersonjr.com

Athens Avenue Podcast: https://www.youtube.com/@AthensAvenue

About the Authors

DR. LARRY L. ANDERSON JR.

Larry L. Anderson Jr. is a North Philadelphia native who now resides in Greater Philadelphia, Pennsylvania. The Lord has blessed him with a wonderful wife, Kim, and three beautiful children, Marquis, Darius, and Gabrielle.

Anderson graduated from Philadelphia Biblical University (Cairn University) with a B.S. in Bible. He has received his Master of Divinity and his Doctorate in Ministry degrees from Biblical Theological Seminary (Missio Seminary). Dr. Anderson became the Sr. Pastor of Great Commission Church in Philadelphia in September 2004. He also serves the Baptist Resource Network as the Director of Healthy Churches and Evangelism, overseeing 350 churches throughout Pennsylvania and South Jersey. Dr. L.A. is the founder and host of the *Athens Avenue Podcast* birthed in the spring of 2023.

To learn more about Dr. Anderson, visit his website at:

http://Dr.LarryLAndersonJr.com

CHRISTINE O. JAMES

Christine O. James is a resident of Greater Philadelphia, Pennsylvania. She has been blessed to wed the love of her life, Paul, and they have three wonderful children, Jason, Joshua and Janine and two grandchildren. Christine holds a Bachelor of Arts in Psychology from Eastern University in St. Davids, Pennsylvania, and a Master's Degree in Counseling Education (M.ED) from Villanova University, located in Villanova, Pennsylvania. She also oversees the Vision and day-to-day activities of CareView Community Church, serving alongside her husband, Paul J. James, who is the Sr. Pastor. Christine James is a facilitator of honest conversations toward wholehearted living. After many years of counseling, teaching, and facilitating others, she has developed a passion for helping people, especially women, to become their authentic selves.

To learn more about Christine and her perspective on wholehearted living, visit her website at **COJames.com**.